WIN TIME

FEARLESSLY TRANSFORMING YOUR SCHOOL

STEPHANIE MCCONNELL
MORRIS LYON

PRINCIPAL PRINCIPLES™ PUBLICATIONS
UNITED STATES OF AMERICA

Stephanie McConnell, Principal Principles
P O Box 26
Leesburg, Texas 75451
www.principalprinciples.net

Book Layout ©2017 BookDesignTemplates.com

Ordering Information:
Quantity sales. Special discounts are available on quantity purchases by corporations, associations, and others. For details, contact the "Special Sales Department" at the address above.

WIN Time: Fearlessly Transforming Your School/ McConnell, Lyon. —1st ed.
ISBN 978-1-7346374-0-3

TABLE OF CONTENTS

Dedication

This book is dedicated to the teachers, students, families, and board members who inspired and challenged me along the way to be better than I was yesterday. Thank you for aiming for excellence, staying focused on results and relationships, and always keeping the promise to have the greatest school on earth.
To all the school leaders who pursue the passion and imagine a better school for their students.
To my family who stands by me and shows up to support with their heart and hands.

-Stephanie

I dedicate this book to my family, thanks to my wife, Holly, and my girls Ally & Lilly, for your continuous love and support. I want to thank my mom and dad for sacrificing and always believing in me. Thanks to all of my colleagues and mentors in my life who have helped to mold me into the person I am today. Thanks to the inspiring teachers, outstanding students, caring parents, and visionary board members that I have worked with and learned from through the years, I cherish the memories. I hope that the experiences in this book, taken from the lessons I have learned, will allow you to elevate your leadership for the benefit of students and educators.

-Morris

It's time to WIN!

—Stephanie

CHAPTER 1

WHAT IS WIN TIME?

by *Stephanie*

The definition of WIN Time is a focus on designing a system of learning that is specific to the students with their needs in mind. It stands for "what I need," also known as a learner-centered approach. In schools today, we hear about personalized learning, individualized learning, and differentiated instruction. All are excellent modes of learning. Understanding the difference between the terms and how they all work, we have developed a blended combination that results in addressing the academic goals of every student. Both the teacher and the student create paths or plans, either as remediation or enrichment.

During WIN time, we can create a curriculum specific to the student's needs by designing targeted instruction correlated with data checkpoints. Students then work on the content and reflect on their learning by creating goals; in the end, they take ownership of their learning. Another avenue is to select best practices and curriculum resources that help students master the state standards. Both routes are effective and produce great success individually. However, creating a blended model provides the liberty to the teachers and staff to create flexible groups and to plan without the dependence on technology and without having to redesign our instructional programs.

I was having a conversation at school with a teacher in which we had a deep discussion about the difference between personalized learning, individualized learning, and what we do on campus. After much brainstorming and debates, she had the most brilliant view of the two terms: personalized and individualized. In her spare time, she creates designer mugs for friends and family. She said I could individualize the mug by putting our school logo on it, or I could personalize each mug and add the monogram or name specific to the buyer. This was a home-run clarification. In our school, we have married the two, creating a learner-centered approach that gives us opportunities to individualize instruction for groups of students, or we can hone in on specific content areas and consider the student's voice and choice.

One-size-fits-all will not prepare our students for the next grade level or the real world. Every student is unique and learns in different ways. In order to guarantee you are meeting every student's needs, you have to use a diverse array of strategies or approaches as opposed to whole group lectures or the one-size-fits-all.

There are years of research that you can read about all the best approaches and paths that lead to better student outcomes when compared to traditional methods. However, our learner-centered approach has proven effective in both school districts in which I implemented the model. In a previous district, we called the model FLEX. It wasn't until my current district that we coined the name WIN.

My previous district encompassed approximately 9 or 10 teachers per grade level. My current campus has 3 per grade level. Regardless of the campus size, the model works.

ELEMENTS OF LEARNER-CENTERED INSTRUCTION

1. Learner-centered instruction contains explicit skill instruction.

2. Learner-centered instruction embraces students knowing their data and encourages students to reflect on what they are able to know and do.

3. Learner-centered instruction is flexible and fluid, both in student groups and content.

4. Learner-centered instruction involves campus-wide collaboration and teamwork.

5. Learner-centered instruction can only happen with great teachers.

6.   Learner-centered instruction places the student at the center of every decision and supports are built around them.

WHY IMPLEMENT A WIN-TIME SYSTEM?

What if the school you lead and walk into each day was able not just to meet students' deficiencies, but you were also able to accelerate their growth?

What if you were able to create study plans that were specific to each student?

What if you were in a great position to make small shifts to move your school from low performing or met standard to an exceptional level of performance, earning your school national recognition?

This is not a sales pitch. This is exactly how we turned our school around and why I'm so passionate about sharing this success with you. I am incredibly fired up to share our story so you can achieve victory too.

This book is unique from other books you may have read. *WIN Time* can be read from the beginning to the end, or you can select the chapter you need at the time and work on the tasks solely in that one chapter. It doesn't matter how you move through the chapters; what matters is that you get to your finish line. Each chapter has a "problem of practice" or POP. If you are not familiar with the process or the term *problem of practice*, don't be embarrassed. Until writing this book, I too didn't know that my very actions and processes on campus actually had a term called *problem of practice.*

A problem of practice, or POP, involves discussion and data to identify an issue. It is typically a description in a few sentences of what the problem is you need to solve. In this description, data is included to support the need to make changes. Each POP also incorporates some general questions to ponder and to guide the discussion and problem-solving process. In essence, guiding your school to think about the challenges and problems the school is experiencing will determine the root cause of the issue, what circumstances are being determined, and steps the school can take to make a greater impact and difference in student learning. As you venture into this process, I urge you to keep in mind that the problem of practice is not to be done by the leader alone in isolation. This process is a collaborative approach done with the staff in full partnership.

IDENTIFYING A PROBLEM OF PRACTICE

Here is the most recent problem of practice from my school this week.

> Increasing the number of students who participate in UIL events and supporting students in achieving higher levels of placement in the academic competitions.
>
> Our placement in academic UIL events indicates that our students are not achieving at the same levels as our surrounding schools in the competition. Low student achievement in areas such as number sense, music memory, and maps, graphs, and charts have been identified. The staff has stated a few causes of low performance as student's unwillingness to stay after school for UIL practice, student scheduling in multiple events causing the student to not have enough in-depth practice in single events, and student incentives to be self-disciplined and persevere during the months leading up to the competition. Another root cause is the inability to attract and retain staff to coach UIL events.
>
> Focus Questions:
>
> How can we create a school-wide UIL model of practice during the school day that will allow more students to participate?
>
> How can we motivate students to persevere and foster self-discipline?
>
> What events are achieving the most success and why?
>
> How can some of the competitive events connect to our everyday classroom instruction?

The UIL committee was formed to discuss the concerns and causes of our lack of higher performance in the UIL events this year. During the meeting, the staff formulated some solutions to consider. The ideas the staff brainstormed supported the school and district efforts. Our next step is to create a school-wide plan that is actionable and is focused on achieving our goal.

This book is not a quick fix to magically transform your school overnight. The strategies and models shared are not to be implemented every now and then or even swiftly until you have all the moving pieces in place and communicated. To have a successful school takes a lot of hard work on everyone's end: administrators, teachers, and students. I certainly don't presume to think you are not aware that everyone has to be willing to make concessions in the classroom in order to produce the desired results. As I said before, we can no longer accept a one-size-fits-all classroom in which every student is given the same material, asked to sit at a desk the entire class period, and the teacher does all the talking and thinking. To get the results you desire, we must be realistic and clear from the very beginning.

Not only is this book filled with strategies on how to develop a system of support for your students, I hope you find it motivating and inspiring to lift your spirits and to give you the courage to battle through the difficult times and to celebrate big through the best of times.

We want you to feel success.

We want you to WIN.

Let's get started.

CHAPTER 2

PLAY TO WIN

by *Stephanie*

"Winning means you're willing to go longer, work harder, and give more than anyone else." Vince Lombardi

The most vital assets in our school are the people: the staff and the students. It is up to us to maximize our most precious resources and to build their capacity every single day. To do that, I know my best chance at making any impact relies on my ability to be an effective leader. As a district or campus leader, we are responsible for so many variables: guaranteeing students grow from year to year, monitoring classroom instruction and performance, maximizing funds, creating a culture of collaboration, facilitating meetings, integrating technology in the classrooms, and keeping up with all the social and emotional needs. I am always feeling like a combination lock, searching for the right numbers in the right order so I can consistently produce results on a regular basis.

Morris and I don't claim to know it all. In fact, I know I don't. However, we have found a few things along the way that have been saving graces to help us move our school from failing to high-performing. In addition, we now have a united staff that is tenacious enough to be unstoppable and determined to succeed.

What is WIN time? W.I.N. stands for "what I need." In this book, we will share systems that allow us to serve all students, regardless of performance level. Equally, we hope this book does the same for you. It will serve your needs as a school leader, giving you exactly what you need regardless of years of experience or skill sets you possess. In fact, we hope to meet your needs exactly where you are. Our goal in writing this book is that leaders at every level will benefit from the insights and practical ideas. In chapter 7, we will share details of the logistics and day-to-day operations of W.I.N., which has not only been a successful practice on my campus for several years, but it is one practice that many school leaders come to observe. Before we set that chapter in motion, let's talk about exactly what brought you to purchasing this book and what you might be currently experiencing.

Every leader is at different levels of leadership and has different philosophies on how to lead, and brings various skill sets and values to the table. You probably know better than anyone else how you learn best. You may be the person who picks up a book and reads it once or listens to a podcast and can immediately start working on creating the school you truly want. Or you might be someone who needs repeated exposure to the process and then weighs your options over a few weeks or months, brainstorms it with a few best friends, and then still overthinks it all together. None of that matters. The only thing that matters can be best shared from Vince Lombardi, "Winning means you're willing to go longer, work harder, and give more than anyone else." So, what exactly are you experiencing this year or seeking answers to?

1. Are you struggling to create systems that serve all students, regardless of performance levels?

2. Are you trying to grasp how to create a vision so powerful that it lights the hearts of everyone on fire?

3. Are you trying to determine what actions will improve your school?

So many school leaders have told me they are not ready to start transforming their school because they don't know where to start. Or they say they have too much going on right now, and they just can't tackle one more thing. I'm going to be completely honest with you right now. You will always have something going on. You are always going to be busy. We have to move from the mindset of *I'm getting ready to get ready*. The driving force to start now or later is best determined by the desire to serve the students sitting in the desks in your classrooms. The students deserve us to start this minute. Think about this for a minute. Where could you be in a few months if you just put a stake in the ground and said **today is the day?** You deserve a win. And most definitely, your staff and students deserve to win.

Let me talk a little truth with you. If you want to be successful at anything in your school, you have to get laser-focused on the one thing you want to succeed at. A massive movement toward your goal means you have to start today. We all have a desire for something. My desire is always to do the very best I can every single day. Like most things, we get what we focus on. Let's map out our winning path right now. Starting is the most difficult part.

PLAYING TO WIN

I am a very competitive person both personally and professionally. My home can get loud really quick when the games come out during the holidays. I know the outcome of every game by knowing if I'm playing to win or playing not to lose. There is definitely a difference. If I am playing to win, I will lay it all on the line and leave no opportunity on the table. If I am playing not to lose, I don't normally take every chance or risk my hand of cards. I tend to be more cautious and at times, I wait for a better hand of cards to be dealt to me. If I'm playing to win, I'm not reckless, but I am definitely more calculated in my behavior. I told you I am competitive. I have noticed that when I am behind in a game, I will take more risks to try and catch up. But when I am several points ahead or even tied in a game, I am extremely cautious and rethink every single card I play. Why would I do this? Honestly, I wasn't even aware of my own behavior until I started writing this book, which just so happens to fall during the holidays. So here I am in the midst of confession and reflection, pondering how and why I wouldn't just step forward and risk falling behind in a game or throwing it all on the table and winning.

This behavior makes me question my behavior when approaching things at school. Am I playing to win or playing not to lose? The answer to this question will give me different outcomes. My challenge for you and me is to find opportunities to grow your school. The way to do that is to take a risk and play to win. You owe this to your students, staff, and community to have a winning team and to build a winning school.

VISUALIZE A WIN

A technique that athletes use to mentally and physically perform and prepare is called visualization. I don't claim to be an athlete, but I do dabble in a jog and an outdoor adventure as often as I can. I have three grown children who compete in Spartan races and many 5K and 15K races just for the fun. When we are together, my daughters enjoy torturing me to a run and not my causal jog. They used the visualization method with me, and it worked. As we were running, I wanted to stop over and over again. They said, "Just run to the tree and you can slow down your pace." The tree remained my finish line and was in my vision. When approaching the tree, my daughter said, "Don't stop, just slow your steps and catch your breath." The next command was to look up and seek the road sign. This was my next point to reach. As we ran, I was instructed to keep my stride in alignment with their steps. I watched their feet hit the payment and I followed in the same momentum. I certainly understand this is not completely what true athletes do because I am no athlete. However, my brain and body performed when the task was given to me in segments. Your brain does not know the difference from winning the event and imaging a win. Each time I reached the destination on the trail or path, I felt a win. I can't help but make a connection to this strategy and think of how it may apply to us as school leaders and educators. We need to visualize a win by seeing ourselves completing a goal and feeling that victory. By training my mind to think strategically, I was able to see it all come together. I could see the steps I needed to take to reach my destination. This method can help us as school leaders to stay motivated and to work harder when times get tough. Compellingly, visualization to me is really just being focused on a dream. It is mind over matter and a bit of brain play. I'm sure you have used visualization many times in your life and never realized it. You may have used this strategy when you were nervous to give a speech or had a little bit of anxiety just getting up in front of a small group of people. Putting yourself in the situation mentally helps you play out the tasks in your head before you do the real thing. Your brain won't know the difference from imagining the speech to actually performing the real one.

Just recently, I watched the movie *Overcomer*. The movie is about a high school basketball coach, John Harrison, who reluctantly coaches cross-country, a sport he doesn't even like. His team is made up of only one student, Hannah Scott. John trains her to win the championship. In the movie, Hannah gets to know her father, who was also a former runner. Visualization was used to overcome the challenges and obstacles not only in Hannah's personal life, but it was used to mentally and physically win a championship. Hannah was allowed to use an earpiece in which her father recorded words of inspiration as she reached every step on the cross-country trail. The words he said stuck with me. He said, "You don't win races with just your legs." It is a mental race because your body will want to quit, but you must push through and focus on what's ahead. We must think like a winner and know that this race we are on belongs to us. We can't be weighed down with negativity and self-doubt. Finish strong and keep your eyes on the finish line and allow yourself the opportunity to feel the win.

WIN IS A VERB

The word *win* shouldn't always be considered a noun. We should think of the word as a verb and be continuously striving for wins every day. Like it or not, we live in a world that keeps score. If winning wasn't important, people wouldn't keep score. There is a winning spirit in all of us. A winning spirit will be your motivation to pursue your goals, and your commitment to the goal will carry you through every day. Our hope for you is to keep that real burn inside of you to take your school to the next level. Your unbridled enthusiasm and burning desire to make a big difference and bring about change will be a ripple effect to the people on your campus. Surround yourself with people who want you to succeed and can help you and your campus feel the wins. Create the right environment on campus where everyone has the opportunity to thrive and everyone celebrates together in the halls. Don't get trapped in the whirlwind of the day-to-day activities that you overlook the meaningful steps your campus has taken this day or this week. Be proud of every step, no matter how big or small. Find your gratitude to appreciate the steps you just made and keep your eyes on the excitement for future wins.

Let's begin to think of actionable steps we can take to solve a real situation on your campus. Gather a school leadership team to help solve the campus problem. Next, begin by identifying the problem. This is a short statement that precisely shares the problem. Write the problem of practice at the top of a piece of chart paper or be able to verbally communicate the problem with your campus team. Explain the problem in great detail so your team fully understands the situation. Provide a list of focus questions so the team can ponder and will help guide the discussion.

PROBLEM OF PRACTICE

This POP centers around *what I need* to create a winning culture. Our problem of practice is included to give you an example and to spark a thought that will lead to an action on your part. In the back of the book, you will find the pages to outline your problem of practice in your school. Use our example as a catalyst or brainstorm with your team to identify a problem on your campus to focus on. Remember, focus on two to three important things and generate a team to help in this effort. Your problem

of practice may take a few weeks or a few months, but most importantly,

outline the problem and practice an actionable plan with your team to

transform your school for a WIN!

How to prioritize when everything is so important: I have so many problems, and I don't know where to start!

A principal was just hired and has been faced with a daunting challenge. The campus was experiencing their fourth principal in four years. Each principal previously stayed only a year for various reasons: promotions in or within the district, reassignment to another position, or retirement. With each change in administration, the campus staff became less engaged and less trusting. Every year, the campus tried to embrace the changes only to find out another year of uncertainty was inevitable. Systems began to fail. Discipline began to rise. Morale was not even a thought because survival was the norm. The data supported the need for a comprehensive schoolwide approach to creating a response-to-intervention system, as well as designing a curriculum alignment process, implementing team building, revamping the discipline plan with clear expectations, and gathering more rigorous instructional resources. As a new principal, where should we begin first? How do we prioritize areas to focus on first?

Focus Questions:

What steps can the school take to drive consistent implementation of changes this year?

In what ways can the staff take on leadership roles to build high-functioning teams and implement positive changes in the areas of need?

What is the first thing to do to set great things in motion?

Is there an opportunity in the day to block off time dedicated to working on the goals? What does that look like?

CHAPTER 3

VISION FOR THE WIN

by *Morris*

"If you tell people where to go, but not how to get there, you'll be amazed at the results." George S. Patton

As we all know, General George Patton was considered a great military leader by many due to his ability to motivate troops under his leadership. Even though his brazen tactics and often vulgar approach was not appealing with everyone, he exhibited courage and gained respect from his troops by leading alongside his soldiers, and he exhibited great leadership skills. When reading his quote, I think of how important it is for the people in any organization or operation to understand where they are going. There is a certain sense of calm and purpose when there is a common vision understood among all those involved. Also, if we as leaders outline where we are headed and what we expect, our staff will work together to achieve the task and have ownership in the process.

As a leader, we will face many obstacles with the organization we have been entrusted to lead. How many times have you encountered a leader who had no vision? I have seen leaders who could address the daily problems and issues around them but had no sense of direction to lead the organization to common ground or greater expectations. Often, if we just watch and listen, we can learn from the leaders around us, both positive and negative. When I reflect on General Patton's quote, I think how unfortunate it is for a school that has a leader who is reactive instead of proactive. In Patton's world, poor leadership could result in death. In the world of education, we are entrusted to make decisions that will impact students for the rest of their lives until death. How can a leader see the issues surrounding their school but not formulate a vision to implement a common direction? When I reflect on my early years, I think how unfortunate it was for my school when I was a reactive leader; only until I understood the power and impact of a well-formed vision did I see my school undergo a systematic transformation.

Visioning is one of the most essential tools of a leader for transformational change, but often, it is the most underutilized or misunderstood task. I have seen so many leaders in my career just "check the box" when it comes to developing a vision and mission. It often happens that we go through the motions to get our list completed instead of taking time to implement powerful opportunities that can have a huge organizational impact. I presume we do these shortcuts, many times, due to a lack of resources and time. However, I have come to a resolution that implementing a thorough and powerful vision will actually move your organization or school at a much quicker pace for change. How? It is all in the WHY.

WHY IS A VISION IMPORTANT?

Just with any child, student, adult or school employee, we all want to know WHY. I think it is embedded in our DNA. Why are we doing this? Why is this a priority? Why do I need to learn this? Why do we have to spend time doing this silly vision when I have papers to grade?

When I first started at Hawkins ISD in the spring of 2016, I knew I had a task ahead of me. The school board president called me the morning after the board meeting to select a new superintendent and said, "Well, we had a long meeting last night, and we decided to offer you the job. You have the most experience, and we felt you would be the best equipped to handle this job." I was thinking in my mind, *what am I getting into here?* I went to the next board meeting to be named the lone

finalist and was granted the honor on a 4-3 vote. There was a heaviness

in the air, and I could tell there were some relationships to be repaired

and teamwork building to be done. So, I began to go to lunch with board

members and staff to listen and learn. I asked WHY so much that my

assistant superintendent at the time said, "You sure do ask WHY a whole

lot." I knew if our school people could not answer why we did certain

things, then we did not have a full understanding of our organization.

I could see right from the start that we had a school full of great people,

great students, and a great community, but as Covey says, "good had

become the enemy of great." It appeared to me that many had become

okay with being okay. A change was brewing, and I had been at the

center of that brewing pot with the split vote of the board. However, I

was happy when they brought me back to be named the superintendent,

and I received a 7-0 vote. So, the visioning work began.

Having the mentality to be okay will not get a school very far when the

state accountability system is progressive. During this time, Texas

transitioned to a new accountability system that no longer gave a "met

standard" to 95% of the schools. We were now going to get letter grades.

During my listen and learns, I had already identified learning and curriculum gaps. We also had limited organizational systems in place, and we had a strong sense of silo teaching. What I mean by silo teaching is we had no professional dialogue; everyone was doing their own thing with nothing close to PLCs, and vertical alignment was nonexistent. We did not fully understand our state standards to the degree in which I was satisfied, nor were we leveling our instructional resources to the appropriate grade. Basically, everyone shut the doors and did their own thing with limited accountability. With no local accountability and the new state progressive accountability on its way, we were headed for a perfect storm.

So, hopefully, you have a picture of the condition of the school in which I had moved. We were fragmented, to say the least, and we did not have an understanding of where we were headed. Please do not take my account of the status of our district as a reflection of poor effort or lack of quality people. We had people working hard and doing what they thought was best for the school, but they had missed the why, and they had a lack of vision. They could see the problems, and they would tackle the tasks from day to day, but they had no plan or vision to correct the path. This idea was confirmed to me later when I had staff open up to me and tell me their true feelings.

So, the storm hit just before the semester break in December of 2016. We received our Texas Education Agency preliminary district ratings. We had a rating of "F." Fortunately, we had been working on our vision, mission and core values the previous months and we had finished our systemic plan. During this process, we had healed some relationships and built teams within our board and on our campuses, so when we received the rating, it presented some urgency, not panic, and it validated some of the concerns I had communicated with the stakeholders. I believe the months we invested in discovering our vision, mission and core values, through the time we spent having professional dialogue and understanding our WHY, helped us launch into an action plan to transform our district. The conversations offered an opportunity for some employees to be heard, and it produced a product in which everyone had ownership. From this point, we implemented a four-year plan and began to look at staffing and placing people in the right positions to expedite the plan. The work completed during the visioning process helped to build teamwork, ownership with a common purpose and a common direction to be able to communicate so that we could understand our WHY. The visioning produced a clear message of where we were going, but the process of visioning was what transformed our school. Often, we shortchange the process due to a lack of resources or time, but the power, in this case, was in the process. Of course, I could have written a vision statement and posted it on the wall, but the process is what helped to pull everyone together, giving us something to rally around. I am convinced our visioning process with quality people is how we went from an F rating to just one point away from an A rating in two years and how Hawkins Elementary was a 2019 National Blue Ribbon School of Excellence for Closing the Achievement Gaps. Our vision: **to be the model of a learner-centered school.**

COMMON MISUNDERSTANDINGS OF VISIONING

To follow our vision, to be the model of a learner-centered school, Stephanie began to open our school to others, so we could demonstrate the systems and practices that had been successful for our students to earn a National Blue Ribbon award. We began to host so many schools that we quickly decided we must manage our visitors so we could continue the learning environment on our campus. We set up monthly walks, but we still had requests for more training. So, Stephanie and I developed an instructional training in which a portion of the day focused on the importance of a strong vision (refer to the back of this book for a link to the course). It was during this training where I learned the common misunderstandings some of our leaders had for school visioning. I realize that many of the leaders attending our training were principals and not superintendents. However, the misunderstanding of visioning confirms to me the lack of visioning in our schools. If visioning were practiced by our central administration, as a process, then our campus leaders would understand the power of the visioning.

The biggest misunderstanding I have seen is the difference between a vision and a mission. We had several questions asking about how these two items differed. If you think about a military operation, any branch of the service, the unit has a clear mission to carry out. They have precise orders and directions to carry out the work in the present. However, the leadership must be prepared for the response of the enemy and have a future-focused idea in mind of achieving the ultimate goal, to win the war. So, the vision is future-minded, and the mission is the daily work in the current time. Many times, when we are in the trenches, we do not see the big picture. It is important to know the big picture while understanding the future-focused idea that we as a team want to achieve. This serves as a standard, a guidepost. It is the leadership's role to reinforce the positive communication of the vision, the goal of the future, the ultimate goal to achieve ...to win the war (keeping with the military theme). The common restatement and reminding of the vision begin to serve as a comfort. It serves as a positive motivator when the work gets hard; it serves as a rallying cry and it serves as a unification of a team working toward a common goal. Whether in a battle for a strategic military post or in shaping students' minds in our classrooms, the work is hard and those in the trenches thirst for a strong visionary leader.

Keeping with the military examples, on vacation we have toured retired navy vessels docked in port. I have always been impressed with the massiveness of the anchor. The anchor is huge with massive chains and motors to raise and lower the anchor in order to keep the vessel grounded. Many leaders fall short in using the vision as an anchor of decision making for their school. The vision should be the anchor for all actions in your school. After all, the vision should be what you want your school to become in the future, so it makes perfect sense that all decisions should be anchored in the vision. If not, then the leader is just reacting to the pressures around them and not moving in a proactive manner. As explained earlier, the vision of the leader is crucial to carry out a successful mission. The military mission has strategies for the different units to follow supported with specific goals and objectives. If the visionary leader has developed a good vision and then uses a backward design model to build a plan down to the goal and objectives, then the plan of attack should be linked together, and the military should work as a seamless machine conquering the vision of the leader. This is where many school leaders miss an opportunity. Many school leaders use the "to-do list" leadership and miss the opportunity of a seamless machine working together for the success of students. When you use the vision as your anchor, you are moving away from the isolation of siloed tasks, and you then are operating your school in a true teamwork mentality.

Other common misunderstandings or missed opportunities include the power of communicating a vision and the benefits gathered through the process of visioning. The process itself is a great team-building activity for any organization. Once a leader builds capacity in their visioning team, the team can be used to facilitate the visioning process on the campuses so everyone can feel ownership. When you provide ownership in a process, the people will support the work. They will also understand the direction of the school and become ambassadors for the school. As mentioned in the military example above, explaining the difference between a mission and a vision, communication of the vision is a powerful leadership tool. A campus leader should take every opportunity to communicate the vision to staff, students and parents. Remember, the vision is a positive future-focused statement that you aspire for your school. So, as with any good habit, when you restate it over and over, it becomes a habit and the students, staff, and parents will begin to believe. Once everyone begins to believe, then the belief will become reality and your vision will be realized.

The final misunderstanding to discuss in this section is the misconception of visioning being a waste of time. We had one leader express to us in a webinar about their frustration with the visioning process. This leader had worked hard and was excited about the process, but they were receiving negative feedback from a teacher about the time it was taking to create a common vision. Unfortunately, some leaders have this same thought process. Often these leaders are the same ones that focus on massive discipline changes and programs rather than investing in engaging classrooms. It is a conundrum. If we focus on the most important thing, there will be a major impact on other important things. I am not saying a quality discipline program isn't important, but as we all know, there is a direct relation to highly engaged classrooms and reduced discipline referrals. I am convinced the same is true for organizational transformation and visioning. If we carry out the visioning process, we will transform our school at a much faster pace. A leader is going to spend their time being reactive or proactive by being a manager or a visionary. At the end of the day, it is your choice, what will that choice be?

WHERE DO I START WITH CREATING A VISION?

As the leader of your school, you should have an idea of the landscape. Earlier in the chapter, I outlined my experience being new to the district and how I gathered information to understand the needs of the school. We had a huge trust issue when I first came to my district, so I knew I had to have a team to develop the vision. I needed a group to help move the vision forward; as they say, there is safety in numbers. If you have been at your school for some time but just need a boost, then hopefully the trust has already been established for you. However, a team to help facilitate the vision development is helpful.

If you struggle where to begin, then begin with the data. Solid decisions will always be based on solid data. In our district, after asking why and reviewing data, I could tell we needed to be standard-centered and learner-centered to ensure everyone received what they needed. It was also obvious that we needed to learn as a staff. I found myself learning how to try to gain trust and to move the organization to transformation. So, the idea of being learner-centered started to take on the meaning of a learner ranging from the student to the superintendent. How can we better prepare students for their future than by modeling learning as education professionals? As educators, we have always verbalized lifelong learning, but our vision embodies the practice.

There are people to help facilitate the creation of the vision, but with the *process* of visioning being the benefit, doing it as a school team is the most effective. Being courageous and having a growth mindset plays a large role in vision development. There are programs and books to help you research the development, but if you as the leader put in the work, the product will be most effective. Lead the charge!

IMPLEMENTING A VISION ON THE CAMPUS LEVEL

One question that has arisen on several occasions in our training is, "I am a principal, but how do I implement a vision on my campus?" The apprehension is understandable. Some central administration teams are very strict and want you to employ a cookie-cutter philosophy, or they may feel like visioning is a waste of time. However, every school has a different culture and every school has a separate team.

If you have a district vision, please do not ignore it or the strategic plan. If the superintendent is the general and the principal is the sergeant, then there is still a direction and a vision to follow, but each principal, just as each sergeant, will have their own group to lead. The whole district much lead in step, but each campus has its own terrain to maneuver, and the goals and objectives may be different. As the superintendent, I encourage my principals to have their own campus vision that links into the district vision. In fact, I encourage my food service director, transportation director, and other departments to have their own vision. The process to me is more than an instructional transformation; it can be an organizational transformation.

In summary, the process is the most important benefit of visioning. The process is why any leader should embrace visioning. The words on a piece a paper can be written, and the box for having a vision can be checked. However, for true transformational visioning, those very words on paper must be embodied by the staff, students, and parents. The vision must be communicated, embraced and practiced. When this happens, transformation happens. Be the visionary leader for your school!

PROBLEM OF PRACTICE

This POP centers around *what I need* to build a vision for your school. Our problem of practice is included to give you an example and to spark a thought that will lead to an action on your part. In the back of the book are pages for you to outline your problem of practice in your school. So, use our example as a catalyst or brainstorm with your team and identify a problem on your campus to focus on. Remember, focus on two to three important things and generate a team to help in this effort. Your problem of practice may take a few weeks or a few months, but it is most important to outline the problem and to practice an actionable plan with your team to transform your school for a WIN!

Build clarity in the direction of the campus and create unity and team-work to complete campus and district goals. Implement the district vi-sion through a campus focused vision and action plan.

There is a lack of clarity in the direction of the campus, which is caus-ing a lack of unity and lack of a clear direction. We have a district vi-sion, but it is not communicated or referenced, and it has been a number of years since it was updated. Research shows that a clear di-rection, a collective process for gathering campus needs from stake-holders and a strategic process for outlining this process will help efficiency and actionable results. Leadership needs to be provided; however, there is a lack of urgency at the district level. The campus will need to develop a comprehensive plan and outline a vision for in-dividualized student growth.

Focus Questions:

How can we build capacity and unity in the campus team?

How do we start the process to build a campus vision?

What is needed to get all stakeholders involved or to get collaborative feedback?

Why do we need a common direction and plan?

What are our needs, and how can we develop milestones to meet the needs for the campus?

What do we value as a school, and what are our boundaries?

How and when will we communicate our vision?

CHAPTER 4

START WITH A WIN

by *Stephanie*

"The real joy in life comes from finding your true purpose and aligning it with what you do every single day." - Tony Robbins

F irst, let's be clear about why you are here. I truly believe we are all here and born with a purpose. I also believe you are in a leadership position because someone believes enough in you to do the job and has confidence that you will do it well. Recognizing this in yourself and taking swift action is not just necessary; it is the essential ingredient for what success is built upon. Tony Robbins says it best in this quote: "The real joy in life comes from finding your true purpose and aligning it with what you do every single day." To succeed as a strong instructional leader, you need to be strategic. This means we must focus on the powerful and most significant priorities that will fulfill our purpose. Without this identified purpose, it's easy to get sidetracked on what other people around you think should be the focus. In addition, it is easy to get caught up in the whirlwind of the day, never moving beyond managing the school. Take it from me who learned it the hard way. You don't want to go all year working toward an unidentified purpose only to find out you had your ladder leaning against the wrong wall. Once you have determined the direction of the WIN for your campus, write it down. Read it every day. This will keep you focused on this purpose. Be determined enough to see the plan through to the end. There is no place for defeat when you are full of determination and focused on your WIN.

PATH TO SUCCESS

Second, identifying the starting line in a race is critical. How does one really know where and when to begin this process? To win any race or to create a successful school, you have to have a game plan. To be successful means you truly know your needs and can meet them with the resources you have been given. As with any situation, first start by identifying what you want to improve in your school. Do you want to increase student achievement in all academic areas? Do you want to improve and boost attendance, or lower discipline referrals, or increase student participation in extracurricular events? First, identify what you are needing to develop. We must strive to fully understand our situation, or school, and our needs. When I was first hired as the principal of my current school, I took an inventory of the campus by speaking to staff members, looking at data charts, and examining my resources. In addition, I wanted to know what we needed to improve. I was also seeking conversations on what we were doing well. Second, choose the best way forward. To be very clear here, the steps you outline must align with the vision, mission, and values of your campus and district. It is easy to forget about this when planning, but if you want to guarantee your win is worthy, it must align with your school's overall purpose.

One of the best ways to achieve your goals is to not just write them down,; goals must be communicated and held as a commitment.

5-STEP PROCESS TO SUCCESS

1. Determine what needs to be improved.
2. Gather all the facts from data and conversations.
3. Map out your path to achieve the goals.
4. Check to be sure goals align to your vision, mission, and values.
5. Make a commitment to yourself and to your staff for the goals.

UNDERSTANDING MY CAMPUS

In 2017, I began my journey as the principal of Hawkins Elementary School (HES). I had previously served many years as a principal of a larger school, but I was excited to begin my journey as a leader under Morris, the co-author of this book. Let me be honest and confess my mindset with you first and foremost. My previous school was almost 600 students. My new campus was half that size. So, I bet you know what I am about to say. "Three hundred students must be easy compared to almost double that." That was precisely my mindset. Shame on me for even thinking that this road would be easy. In a smaller school, yes, we have fewer students. Still, we also have less of everything else: no assistant principal, less funding, and no extra staff members such as directors, assistant superintendents, and so on. Small school leaders wear many hats and rely on the superintendent of the school far more. We wear the hat of truancy officer, disciplinarian, instructional leader, and coordinator of all events.

So, the day I began my journey as the leader of HES, I began my path of success with a game plan. I asked questions, and I asked more questions. I dug into filing cabinets. I ran reports. I opened every closet and took inventory, and I audited all instructional materials and classroom arrangements. Conclusions were being drawn from all the facts. What I found was surprising and eye-opening. I understood clearly that the staff members thought the students were the best part of the campus. The teachers longed for the spirit of the campus to be revived and hoped for the community to be fired-up for the students playing on the fields, courts, and in the classrooms. I realized that our closets were overstocked with textbooks and resources in hopes of being the fixer of all the academic needs. The stacked reports in the filing cabinets evidenced the need to assess, but an action plan based on the data had not been created. I call this data-rich and action poor. The staff members all agreed that discipline had been overlooked for so long that students had become complacent with their own academic future. Some of the reasons for high discipline resulted in a lack of systems for positive behavior supports, student services, and a discipline management plan in place. Other reasons for high discipline were due to a lack of student engagement and rigor in the classrooms. In addition, the campus had no systems in place for response-to-intervention instruction(RtI). Students were lifers in the multi-tiered system of Tier 3. Students were being referred to special education and dyslexia at high rates with very little understanding of how to close the achievement gap prior to the referral. Teachers also recognized the lack of leadership over the years that had also impacted the problems on campus. The staff simply did not have the power to bring about the changes to move the school out of failure.

All this seems quite overwhelming for one person. Therefore, I knew I would never try and tackle this alone. To make the changes the campus needed, I rallied around teachers on campus who could help create ripple effects with me.

CREATING YOUR WIN

The achievement of meeting one goal changes everything. This holds true professionally and personally. Think about that for just a minute. When you meet your goal of running a 5K, or of losing 20 pounds, or of completing your master's degree, or of eating more healthier options, tackling these goals makes it possible to accomplish more. You and your campus need to feel the success of a win. No matter the size of the goal, breaking through the finish line is something that changes your campus. It brings confidence, encouragement, and new opportunities for hope. It is gratifying to witness every success or win along the way. It is even more gratifying to witness teachers and staff move from spectators to taking on leadership roles. Moreover, it is exhilarating to witness teachers, staff, and students move from being interested to being committed. The staff and students have transformed from participating only when it is convenient to actively engaging and accepting no excuses and to holding each other accountable. The campus has transformed from isolated teaching to open doors and conversations. It has been a full 360-degree transformational experience, or in the words of the students on the campus, we have "put a ring on it." We are forward thinkers who focus on what's working instead of constantly focusing on what's broken. We look at our possibilities instead of our weaknesses. We problem-solve solutions instead of showcasing our past failures.

I still remember a big success the teachers and students experienced. On January 15, 2019, Morris and I gathered all staff members together to let them know the campus was nominated by the Texas commissioner of education as a National Blue Ribbon School. Unbeknownst to us at the time, less than one year later, the campus would be the recipient of this prestigious award. As we all gathered in the room, I could tell the staff was rather nervous about whatever speech was about to be shared. I don't typically hold after-school staff meetings. I have found it very difficult to have everyone in attendance with staff members having after-school activities and working around their own family needs. However, I made every attempt to stress the importance for everyone to attend this staff meeting. Those who could not attend came to me throughout the day, asking for insight on what they would be missing. I was the keeper of the secret and made certain not to tell anyone prior to the meeting. I received emails and text messages asking me if I was resigning because it was not common for us to have after-school meetings. So I can definitely say, the build-up of the announcement was grand. I arranged the room so they could all see the short presentation. The presentation was needed because I knew not everyone in the room would understand the level of greatness of being nominated for a Blue Ribbon Award. I explained it as the Oscars of education, a Super Bowl Championship, a gold medal at the Olympics, and a Medal of Honor. After this explanation, they were certainly excited just to be nominated, but even more so to accomplish this recognition. We explained in order to receive the award next year, we would need to be able to sustain our student's growth again on state assessments plus submit an essay showcasing a snapshot of our school. Prior to ending our meeting, we all committed to making our best effort in reaching this goal. We had a focus and a big audacious dream. #ChampionsWearBlue was our hashtag and our mantra, from that moment forward.

Celebrating accomplishments along the way is a powerful way to rally the troops. It sends a message to those who are meeting the goals and embracing the vision to stay motivated through the good times and bad times, but it also sends a subtle message to those who have not jumped on board. No matter how big or small your accomplishments, they must be celebrated. They must be communicated in a big way. Never underestimate the power of a compliment, a note in a teacher's mailbox, or even a morning pep talk. I will end with one amazing Spartan quote to inspire you and to hopefully give you the courage and motivation to celebrate your own victory today. "The warrior who sweats more in training, bleeds less in war." There will be days when you stumble. Get up. There will be days when you can only take small steps.

Take them anyways. There will be days when it's hard to find inspiration in the midst of resistance and in the face of constant failure. Look deep. In this marathon of transforming your school, all that matters is that you keep going. This, my friend, is how you turn your goals into reality.

PROBLEM OF PRACTICE

This POP centers around *what I need* to create a path to success. Our problem of practice is included to give you an example and to spark a thought that will lead to an action on your part. In the back of the book, you will find pages to outline your problem of practice in your school. Use our example as a catalyst or brainstorm with your team to identify a problem on your campus to focus on. Remember, focus on two to three important things and generate a team to help in this effort. Your problem of practice may take a few weeks or a few months, but most importantly, outline the problem and practice an actionable plan with your team to transform your school for a WIN!

Made a Plan; Failed to Act

The whirlwind of the day-to-day operations of the school can hinder us from accomplishing our goals. The district and campus teams created comprehensive schoolwide plans for the year, but at the start of every day, the intention to act upon these plans fell short. The activities consuming the day seem urgent and often time-consuming to handle. These very activities are preventing the principal from accomplishing any of the campus goals.

Focus Questions:

How can we create a system of accountability to guarantee a concentration on what's most important?

What areas of the day-to-day operations can be automated or delegated to allow the principal to follow through or to follow up on the goals?

What can we do to reduce the amount of time spent on the areas that are consuming the majority of the day?

CHAPTER 5

MORALE FOR THE WIN

by *Stephanie*

"The common denominator of success—the secret to success of
every person who has ever been successful—lies in the fact that
they formed the habit of doing things that failures don't like to
do."-

Albert E.N. Grey

Discomfort is an uneasy feeling that causes anxiety. Transforming your school will not only cause you discomfort, but the entire campus body will be very vulnerable to this as well. A great school doesn't become great overnight. It requires hard work. In fact, this work will require everyone to do what many don't want to do. I'm really not the kind of person who practices voluntary discomfort. I have to push myself to work through it and to step forward in the hard times. The first step to achieving any type of success is understanding the secret of success or having that game plan in place. In the words of Albert E.N. Grey, "The common denominator of success lies in the fact that they formed the habit of doing things others didn't like to do." Honestly, I couldn't say it any better. It is true, yet it sounds so simple. Despite the excuses, you prevail. Despite your limitations, you master it.

I will never forget the message and video of Dick and Rick Hoyt. The father competed in the Ironman Triathlon with his handicapped son in 1989. It included a 2.4-mile open-water swim, 112-mile bike ride, and a 26.2-mile marathon. Now, I don't know about you, but I struggle running a 5K. Team Hoyt could have easily quit. They could have easily had the excuse of the obvious obstacles of being the first disabled person to compete and complete an Ironman triathlon. They pushed through the pain. They did what most of us are not willing to do. They formed a habit of success. Team Hoyt had a purpose that was incredibly strong enough to make them relentless and unstoppable.

My goal, and I'm sure it is yours too, is to lead with purpose. Leading with purpose and the right vision identifies a great leader and is a predictor of goals being obtained. You might be thinking, *what does leading with purpose have to do with morale?* Your purpose, and your ability to lead your team toward this purpose, inspires the team to give their all. It is important for leaders to dig into what their purpose is and how it shapes the school. When everyone is connected as a unit, a team, and a tribe, we all thrive. That connection is even more powerful when everyone is working toward the same purpose. I have studied schools that are making great strides. Schools that are purpose-driven are winning. In the midst of all this purpose-driven activity or lack thereof, morale is at play. When we lead with purpose and every decision being made is intentional and well-orchestrated, the potential to improve your school is limitless.

Just a few days ago, Morris said that as administrators of the district, we must lose ourselves. Our purpose here is something bigger than me. It is about wanting to make a difference and to do for others— to help, to give, and to serve. This purpose serves a bigger mission. Just think about this for a minute. When we understand our purpose, you can touch the lives of others in significant ways. Who wouldn't want that kind of culture or morale resonating throughout the school?

So I ask you, what are you doing as a leader that showcases your ability to lead with purpose? Are your teachers and students motivated and engaged in the school? Are your students achieving wild success and graduating ready to change the world?

Dick Hoyt's purpose was to allow his disabled son the opportunity to participate in something that he could never physically do for himself. In doing so, he captured inspiration and victory for millions around the world to experience and celebrate with him. His purpose to lead his son across the finish line was accomplished against many odds. Every step he took was with purpose, and every decision being made was intentional and well-orchestrated. With that kind of winning attitude, the potential to succeed is limitless.

PUSHBACK FROM STAFF

Pushback is something that will cause a great amount of chaos. It not only keeps the school from moving forward, but it is also a downer for everyone. Let's face it: some people truly prefer to march to the beat of their own drum. They will sit back and discredit those who are making great gains. Their body language represents an unpleasant disposition. In these moments, I have to practice the "quick to listen and slow to speak" method. It is best to listen to their viewpoints. Over the years, I have found that listening to their concerns uncovers miscommunication about the vision or goals or a lack of skill or resources to accomplish the goal. Giving the individual the opportunity to share their concerns helps the staff member feel valued, heard, and appreciated. It also helps to reiterate where we are going and allows you an opportunity to offer support. What you can't do during this time is to change the goal or you will be giving this staff member an opportunity to opt-out or to take a back seat.

RESISTANCE TO CHANGE

There is always one person on the campus who will be difficult. You know exactly who they are, and everybody on campus knows them too. Let's face it: most people prefer stability over change. It's comfortable, and there are no uncertainties when you are never faced with a challenge or disruption in your daily routine. If you are ready to make some changes on campus, it is a given that you will have some resistance from someone. However, we can give you some suggestions right now to get ahead of that opposition. In my experience, sometimes the change can be eased with a few steps from the leaders.

COMMUNICATE CHANGE EFFECTIVELY

Communication is key. No one likes surprises. Being transparent and explaining why the change is necessary is critical. It helps your staff buy-in to the change. Communication should not just be one way. Let your staff have an opportunity to ask questions. I remember the day I met with my staff about the new WIN system on campus. I thought of every question they would have, and I addressed the issues prior to them asking. My campus may be just like yours. They like visuals. I gave them just that in a PowerPoint with graphics. The PowerPoint explained everything from the who, what, why, where, and how it was all going to take place. In the end, I opened the room up for questions. They had very little because I had covered every angle. The staff left the meeting with something in hand, as well. It served as a reference in case they got home and replayed the details out in their head; it gave them something they could easily refer to. I believe communication is key—both written and verbal. It front-loads everything when it comes to massive change.

HERE WE GO AGAIN

The second reason a campus experiences a lot of resistance is because of too much change all the time. I know my campus experienced that prior to my leadership and Morris's too. The district was notorious for purchasing the next best thing to save the campus and to close the achievement gap. They didn't realize that programs can't fix poor student progress, but systems can. My advice is to think about your decisions and lead with intention. Don't be so quick to jump on every new product or idea that comes through. What works for my campus may not work for yours and vice versa.

DEALING WITH COMPLACENCY

Complacency is my biggest pet peeve. Have you realized the word complacency even has the word "place" in it? Staff members who are complacent with the way things are and the way things have always been give me such anxiety. I have to remind myself that maybe they are complacent not because of non-compliance, but maybe they are complacent because they have lost their spark. If so, I can definitely combat bringing the spark back to the building.

Here are a few strategies to help with complacency:

1. Boost the campus morale with some monthly teambuilders, treats, and words of encouragement.

2. Create meaningful ways to get the staff engaged in leading the school. Giving your teachers the opportunity to lead creates significance and engagement.

3. Celebrate! Give your staff something to look forward to. Recognize individuals who go above and beyond.

After coauthoring two books on the topic, I certainly know a little about morale boosting and creating a positive culture. It is time consuming. However, the benefits of doing so are grand. If you face resistance, pushback and complacency in your school, remember the quote from Grey, "The common denominator of success—the secret to success of every person who has ever been successful—lies in the fact that they formed the habit of doing things that failures don't like to do." Face your obstacles head on. When the odds are stacked against you, it is your decision that will change everything. My hope is that you stay resilient and tackle the things that others are too scared to do.

PROBLEM OF PRACTICE

This POP centers around *what I need* to boost morale and gain higher

student achievement. Our problem of practice is included to give you an

example and to spark a thought that will lead to an action on your part.

In the back of the book, you will find pages to outline your problem of

practice in your school. Use our example as a catalyst or brainstorm with

your team to identify a problem on your campus to focus on. Remember,

focus on two to three important things and generate a team to help in

this effort. Your problem of practice may take a few weeks or a few

months, but most importantly, outline the problem and practice an

actionable plan with your team to transform your school for a WIN!

Creating relevance and meaning when staff morale drops.

Certain times of the year, the staff experiences burnout. Tensions run high, patience is thin, and students and teachers are equally tired. The staff's well-being can't be left to chance. By analyzing and reflecting on what is happening during each month, I have noted that October and February tend to have lower morale. Student discipline is higher, and teachers are challenging students with more rigorous instruction.

Focus Questions:

How can the leaders of the school build trust and improve morale?

Brainstorm ways the staff responds and seems energized and uplifted by morale boosters.

What evidence do we see as a positive connection between staff engagement and morale levels?

What activities can be intentionally planned during the lower morale months?

CHAPTER 6

SYSTEMS FOR THE WIN

by *Morris*

"A spider's web is stronger than it looks. Although it is made of thin, delicate strands, the web is not easily broken."

~ E.B. White *Charlotte's Web*

SYSTEMS-BASED APPROACH

The Merriam-Webster definition of *a system* is "a regularly interacting or interdependent group of items forming a unified whole." When we think about systems, the solar system or the digestive system might be the first things that come to mind. Both systems have items that work together to form a unified whole. The system that really made a connection for me in regard to a systems-based approach was when I ran across an article in *Quanta Magazine* titled "The Thoughts of a Spiderweb," by Joshua Sokol. The article explained the research done by a Brazilian biologist Hilton Japyassu. The article outlined a theory regarding the cognitive ability of the spider and how it uses its web as a system. The adaptation of the spider's web to be more useful by the spider dropping threads of the web down to the floor or by stretching horizontal strands across a path to entrap insects shows the adaptation to the environment.

While the article went on to argue the points of cognition of spiders and octopus, etc., my mind wandered back to the spider web. The article explained how the spiders would react to the researcher's removal of a portion of the web, or how the spider would adapt by extending the strands of the web to cover more area or to "fish" for insects. The spider was building a system and then adapting to environmental factors to adjust or modify the system to achieve the results desired. No, I am not comparing the spider to a preying administrator or vice versa, nor am I trying to push the research of Japyassu in saying that spiders have advanced cognitive skills. However, I'm interested in the fundamental ability or basic instinct of a system being used as a tool. We use the spider's web example in many of our tools in education, such as the world wide web or the web graphic organizer, so I guess it is a reasonable connection to use the web as an example to explain a systems-based approach.

While we didn't have this web design in our minds when implementing our systemic design, it turns out that we have linked our systems with that type of redundant support and accountability. Please, do not think that we have achieved perfection in the instructional systems we have in place. Much like a spider would repair the web after a strong wind, so are we in regard to our educational systems-based approach. We are continually refining and trying to make things better. I think this refinement has become conditioned in educators. So, like the spider, we are continuously adapting our system to extend that strand to our kids who are struggling. Of course, our vision is to extend the strand to pull them out of a struggling situation and to help them achieve academic growth (we do not share the ill intent of the spider).

Our systems have been formed over the course of the last four years, but we continually refine so they do not turn into cobwebs. We want a thriving reflective system that is going to achieve its purpose while being flexible enough to absorb the challenges that come its way. There must be enough connection points in our systems that when it does suffer a break, we can hold up our "web" until we have time to repair it, which in most circumstances, makes it stronger.

In the first years of implementation, much like the basis of a stronger web, I knew we needed to be anchored with a strong foundation. As we all know, the foundation, or standards, of our learning are given to us by our great state agency, which are developed through their vetting systems. So, we as a district had to go back to the foundation in order for us to build a strong set of systems; we had to go back to the standards. If we do not understand the importance and the depth of our standards, it does not matter what systems are in place; they will not be effective. Thinking about a spider's web that isn't anchored properly, it isn't going to last long just by the mere lack of connection points. You might be thinking to yourself, *well, that is a no-brainer.* If so, then why are schools not focusing on the standards? Why are so many schools and districts just trying to pile on the latest and greatest program as the "silver bullet" to fix the issue? In our case, we had a whole arsenal of "silver bullets," but there was a foundational problem with the delivery of the standards: lack of knowledge, lack of depth, lack of alignment or just inconsistency in performing the task asked in the standard. I am not saying that one should avoid purchasing resources or products. We purchased an online component to help us with the alignment and pacing of the state standards once we knew that was our foundational need and the anchor point to start building from. There is a difference in having a system and purchasing a product or resource to meet your needs than not knowing your need or not having a system and purchasing a product as a fixer.

From the foundation began the building of systems to encourage student and staff success. Remember, we were moving toward our vision to be a learner-centered school. Stephanie came in during year two, and she implemented a much needed RTI system, which will be discussed in detail in Chapter Seven. This was a key need to addressing the gaps in our student population. This also added the structure of a system that allowed teachers to address the gaps in learning. During this year, we also implemented a systematic formative assessment and a system to track data. As I said earlier, this looks much different than it did the first year since we continue to make refinements to improve our processes. Along with this, we began our first system that encouraged reflection and organizational planning—our instructional rounds. The instructional rounds allowed us to have conversations that revolved around the work and not hold administrative meetings in a boardroom removed from the learning taking place in the classrooms. These professional conversations revolving around the strengths of our campuses and areas we needed to address were crucial in moving us forward. How many times have we sat in a room in an admin meeting discussing what needs to be fixed instead of being immersed in the work where you are able to see the lessons unfold before your eyes? Of course, these walks were never evaluative; they merely provided an avenue for us to gather ideas and thoughts of what we needed to do as a campus or as a district. From this process, we gathered valuable information that allowed us to improve the development of our staff and to make some changes that helped contribute to our 2019 National Blue Ribbon Award of Excellence.

Year three was about implementation to strengthen our delivery of the state standards through a reflective practice model, which we called our "hawk walks." Through our reflective practice model, we had a tool that allowed us to help ensure the standards were taught at the rigor expected in the state standards, Again, this was another strand in the web to help strengthen and ensure mastery of the standard other than a formative assessment. We could use the data from our hawk walks along with data from our instructional rounds and cross-reference to see areas to focus on while we still had time to address the learning before the final state assessment.

I assume this is as good a spot as any to share thoughts regarding our current state of accountability. I, along with most of our staff are very competitive, so we want to WIN at everything we do. Our charge, as educators, is the transfer of knowledge, and that knowledge is determined through our state standards. The validity of any test created can always be argued, and there are challenges with our standardized tests. At the end of the day, our students, school, community, and job will be measured through "our" academic performance. You can say it's not, but it is. I have seen it over and over again. Instead of preaching the state assessment, we focus on mastery of standards and on understanding what task the standard is asking us to master. If we can understand the standard and have the students perform the task asked to be achieved, then the assessment will not be a challenge (assuming the validity part is in play). The conversations should revolve around how we are going to show the state how much we know when we approach the testing season. If we build up our kids and pour into them our love and heart for knowledge, they will perform in life or on a test. We address the standards and the assessment, but our campuses should also include arts, recess/PE, computer and band to ensure we produce not only a student who can perform when expected but also a well-rounded citizen. So, we can like or dislike state assessments, but it is part of the package, and most people, I think, embrace fair accountability.

This year, year four, we are refining and formulating a new vision for our schools. We want to remain current and remain on track for the community and students. We must ensure that we are strengthening our systemic web of learning to be the best we can be for our students.

Reflection questions:

1) What systems do you have to ensure a web of security for your students?

2) How can you build systems to ensure no student is left behind?

3) What refining do you need to do with systems in your school?

4) What system is missing in your school and how do you envision addressing it?

5) Do you have resources supporting your needs and system, or do you have some silver bullets?

BARRIERS TO IMPLEMENTING INSTRUCTIONAL SYSTEMS

As with any new implementation, there is going to be pushback and a sense of distrust and uncertainty, especially if you are new to the school and you have not had time to build relationships. Relationships with people will help when it comes to implementing new ideas or a new vision. Covey has a book titled *The Speed of Trust,* and there is so much power in this theory. If you have that trusting relationship, the speed of implementation is going to be faster.

The barrier you face in implementing systems is going to depend on what is missing from the equation of change. If there is not a plan or a vision, then the staff might experience confusion. In order to move an organization, there must a sense of direction and a place you are heading. If a vision is nonexistent, then everyone will implement their own idea of what the organization needs, creating a silo effect. This will result in each department and or campus doing their own thing with no common goal.

If you do not provide the development of the staff, then this can cause a sense of uneasiness or stress. I had a summer job once when I was 18 years old, in a factory running a wire machine. This large machine would spit out cardboard tags in numerical order while a wire was tied to the tag. My job was to grab the tags on the 25s, put a rubber band on them and put them in a box; all at a speed of about 25 tags every 10 seconds. When I was told, on my third night, that I was expected to run the machine by myself the following night, I did not show back up to work. I was so stressed about messing up the machine that I was afraid to go back to work. I later learned that they were supposed to give me a minimum of three weeks of training before having me fly solo. The company was short-handed, so they were trying to push me much faster than I was prepared to go. While I am embarrassed at my poor choice to not return to work, I have often used this lesson so I will not make the same mistake as a leader. My goal is always to ensure our staff are well trained and have the availability of resources they need to grow and to be prepared to take on the field of teaching.

Our systems of sustainability will be discussed in Chapter 11, but we have tried for a number of years to begin a mentor program. Once a solid set of instructional systems is in place, there is a need for training so they will remain sustainable as new employees enter the organization. We had a vision of a solid mentor program; however, due to the lack of an action plan and resources, we had failed attempts and multiple false starts with our mentor program. When resources are not available, the onset of frustration is felt among the ranks. We try to build in a contingency in our budget when we can, so when a needed item comes up, we are able to purchase it. My goal is to try to reduce the frustration level in the administration whenever possible. As a systems administrator, I want to be able to provide resources when a resource or a desperate need for students is presented by fellow administrators.

THE ROLE OF THE SYSTEMS ADMINISTRATOR

"What's miraculous about a spider's web?" asked Mrs. Arable. "I don't see why you say a web is a miracle; it's just a web."

"Ever try to spin one?" asked Dr. Dorian. ~ E.B. White

In *Charlotte's Web*, Mrs. Arable was concerned for Fern and went to discuss her concerns with Dr. Dorian. She didn't feel it was normal for Fern to be having conversations with farm animals. Dr. Dorian had heard about the webs at the farm and thought that Fern was just being a kid and that she would be fine. I do think this excerpt sums up the creation of systems in your school. An outsider might think, *well, that is simple, just teach the standard, do a walkthrough, and the kids will learn because the teacher is teaching. No problem there.* Like the quote at the beginning of this section illustrates, unless you have been the systems administrator, most individuals making the suggestions have never created a system for learning; they have never spun a web!

In summary, the role of the administrator is somewhat like the spider tending the web: be diligent, be aware of the data the system is telling you, help to patch the system when help is needed, use the data you have to make the system better, be attentive to staff and listen for their concerns and needs, be a visionary and lead the campus to the direction of excellence. Even as a young administrator, I did not understand the full dynamic of good systemic design. I would focus on the crisis of the day and not plan for the future. I did not realize that investing a small amount of time every day to developing systems would return a great amount of time to me in the future. We have invested into many current campus systems that would have saved me so much time earlier in my career had I understood the interconnection and strength in good systems to support the journey of a student learner and to strengthen not only the teacher but myself as well.

PROBLEM OF PRACTICE

This POP centers around *what I need* to build school systems. Our problem of practice is included to give you an example and to spark a thought that will lead to an action on your part. In the back of the book are pages for you to outline your problem of practice in your school. So, use our example as a catalyst or brainstorm with your team and identify a problem on your campus to focus on. Remember, focus on two to three important things and generate a team to help in this effort. Your problem of practice may take a few weeks or a few months, but most importantly, outline the problem and practice an actionable plan with your team to transform your school for a WIN!

There is a need for educational systems to develop a peer accountability process to encourage rigorous delivery of the state standard, a process for reflective practice, a plan for individualized growth and a comprehensive link between the systems used.

There is a silo effect on our campus, where everyone is doing their own things with no continuity of services or delivery of standards from one grade to the next. The state standards are not followed consistently, if at all. Individual teacher "pet projects" take precedent over a systemic curriculum or alignment of the standards, causing significant gaps in student learning. The trust between administrators and teachers is nonexistent, and there is an "us versus them" mentality that causes separation from administration and among some teachers. Student performance is suffering, and morale deficiencies are causing staff turnover and a lack of a professional atmosphere. Staff development and current practices have been hindered due to the lack of resources and proper assessment of needs and direction.

Focus Questions:

Where to start? What is the root of the cause, and how will a WIN be established?

What action will start building trust with the staff?

How do we build a vertical alignment?

How do we build capacity in the staff?

What actions will start to build buy-in and ownership?

How can a professional dialogue become established?

CHAPTER 7

LEARNER-CENTERED FOR THE WIN

by *Stephanie*

I was having a full-on cry—a one-time-a-year kind of cry. You know the one where your mascara is beyond repair. This monumental cry was happening in my car in front of the school. That seems to be my cry zone. For someone who never gets way too emotional, I lost all sense of control as the tears streamed down my face.

Why was I crying?

I felt like I was failing miserably as a principal. My campus seemed to always perform satisfactorily. I know you may be reading this and thinking, *what's wrong with being an acceptable campus?* Many principals would love to be out of low-performing status and reach a satisfactory rating. For me, I wanted more. I was committed to my school and motivated beyond just meeting compliance and being average. I love to dabble in curiosity and flirt with risks. I knew I could do better as a leader. I didn't need to be dangled or enticed by any extrinsic factors. I am motivated by my own desire to serve and to lead a high-performing school—a school in which the staff love their job and students are excited to walk through the doors.

In my car (after my meltdown and two-year-old fit), I had a pep-talk with myself. It was in that moment that I realized I had to create a plan. This was no ordinary plan that just involved what I was going to do. I knew it involved the entire school to take action. I had to empower my staff to make decisions and to help me build a new intervention and acceleration model in the school. How was I going to do this? I have never experienced any other method of a school system other than the traditional model of students receiving the same material at the same rate, and those who are achieving below standard are assigned tutoring. This model was not working and would never move the campus beyond being average. But more than that, I had students who were being left behind. Students were struggling and working below grade level, trying to survive in a classroom in which all they had was hope. For my highest performing students, they were not being challenged or expected to do more than anyone else. In the end, whatever was to come over the next few weeks would leave us stronger, better, and wiser than we were then.

We were textbook-driven, and lesson plans supported that finding. We had workbooks and worksheets, and desks were arranged for teacher-led lessons.

I began researching successful schools and reading endlessly about best practices. I spent hours each day calling other school leaders and taking notes on the contributing factor to their successful school. I analyzed my journal to determine one commonality. The commonality was that the school was putting students' needs first and revamping their master schedules to support students' educational paths.

I wondered if I could create a master schedule that allowed students to be served intervention and accelerated services during the school day instead of before or after school tutorials. *What if? Could it be done?*

I knew I didn't want to create a system in which students were being pulled from core classes and then returning to class and falling behind. This would defeat the purpose and only intensify the gaps in learning.

I gathered the team leaders of each grade level together and opened my heart to showcase my desire to brainstorm this plan. After much brainstorming, we created FLEX. FLEX is not an acronym, which is surprising since everything in the school system revolves around an abbreviation. FLEX meant we would be flexible in our day and provide students a 30-minute session to accelerate their instruction or intervene on their instruction.

In looking back and reflecting on this change, it was the catalyst to not just venture into revamping a master schedule, but it was the launch of many transformations to come.

It all sounds like a fabulous plan, but we had a few trials and tribulations along the way. The biggest was that, since we only had 30 minutes of FLEX, some students needed intervention in both reading and math. Our model did not account for the ability to serve both subjects simultaneously. The students would spend six weeks in one content area and switch to the other content area. When this happened, some students would make an academic slide in the other subject. Despite this concern, we only had 30 minutes in the master schedule to be able to do this, so we worked through the pitfalls as best we could.

It wasn't until my current school district that I was able to construct a master that was learner-centered focused and incorporated both reading and math.

WIN TIME was born.

A LOOK AT WIN AT MY SCHOOL

WIN time stands for "what I need." We are simply doing just that. We are giving students what they need during the school day without the students being pulled from instructional time and falling behind. WIN time includes two 30-minute back-to-back times, which allows students to be served in both reading and math. Let me break it down more for you below in greater detail.

WHO

STUDENTS

Learner-centered instruction is flexible and fluid, both in student groups and in content.

This is a school-wide system, so every student goes to WIN groups either as an intervention or remediation student or as an enrichment student. Each student is unique and thoughtfully placed in the flexible groupings as determined by their data checkpoints. We make it a point to move students; this is not always based on a calendar or timeline. We move students based on their performance. We all learn at different rates. Why hold every student to a timeline? In most cases, we have a calendar in which students are rearranged after an in-depth study of the data reports. But there are always those outliers that require us to make swift movement prior to a set date on a calendar.

The content may not always be the same with every group and every day of the week. The bottom line is that we use a rich curriculum that fully engages students. Students are in small groups working directly with teachers. Students are not working independent on busywork, or completing missed assignments, or redoing classwork for a higher grade. This is a time for intensive assistance in which the teacher provides a lesson targeting individuals or groups of students that helps students continue to progress. WIN time is a priority, and instructional time is protected.

> *Learner-centered instruction places the student at the center of every decision, and supports are built around them.*

Placing the student at the center of every decision and building supports around them doesn't mean the student makes decisions on their own. It simply means we consider the students when we plan lessons and when we make decisions about the school as a whole, and we design supports that give students exactly what they need to learn. In order to do that, we must really know our students. As I said, each student is unique and brings experiences and conditions that may hinder or enhance their own learning. Our challenge is to do a deep dive into each individual student to use that information for the betterment of the student.

TEACHERS AND STAFF

No system will work without a dedicated staff backing it. This WIN-time system is only as good as the teachers implementing it. The reason we have been successful at this method is because we have hardworking men and women putting in the time analyzing data, planning intensive instruction, and communicating the outcomes with parents.

> *Learner-centered instruction involves campus-wide collaboration and teamwork.*

Invite your teachers to sit at the decision-making table. We have committees and teams for campus-level discipline, academics, and district-level teams. Who better to make decisions for the students than the very people who really know them best: the teachers serving students daily. Collaboration times can be during common planning times, through professional learning communities, and campus committees and teams. We need teachers and staff members to collaborate about WIN time in order to better plan lessons for students served by multiple staff members, to share resources, and to problemsolve. Ultimately, when we work together as a team, we are not only fostering collegiality and preventing teachers from teaching in isolation, but we are building a stronger system that improves student learning.

On my campus, we have common planning every Wednesday. During this time, we discuss lesson plans and break apart our state standards. Other times, we spend the hour reviewing our data, or we have a book study discussion or participate in classroom instructional tours as a team. Relationships are formed when the staff members are given the opportunity to connect, discuss, and brainstorm together. It is a healthy partnership that builds stronger values, commitments, and accountability to one another.

Do the teachers in your school have an opportunity to collaborate, make decisions, and take action?

Based on my own experiences and professional opinion, I believe that school change is only possible when the adults take responsibility for changing our practices. These very practices and actions can ensure that all students learn. Change and the ability to take action does not happen in the absence of collaboration. We cannot and will not make sustainable change by making all the decisions as a school leader and not allowing the staff to sit at the table. Isolation is not a model of excellence we want to have in our schools. Instead, collaboration can be one of the most effective leverages for school improvement you can easily implement today. *It is the key to improving student learning.*

Learner-centered instruction can only happen with great teachers.

We must invest in our staff. Invest in their capacity to teach, and grow teachers professionally. Invest your time getting to know your staff and building a better partnership and relationship with each and every one of them. Both are equally important in building a successful school. We need teachers to be the experts in their content areas. This is achieved by investing in professional growth opportunities and by building a positive work environment. In the end, we will have greater efficiency and better student outcomes.

This year, we created Hawk Academy, which is our district's mentoring program. Hawk Academy gives our new employees an opportunity to learn from more experienced teachers throughout the year. We allow time for the early career teachers to observe in the veteran teachers' classrooms, and veteran teachers observe in the early career teachers' classrooms to provide feedback. Beginning teachers need time to learn the skills of teaching, but they also need the opportunity to learn about district initiatives. Each month, we have a coffee chat before the start of the day. This coffee chat is a short 30-minute time to provide a presentation or round table discussion on topics such as dealing with discipline, motivating students, creating a teacher website, student engagement, and so many more topics.

A WIN-time system that supports our students can only be as great as the people implementing it. Human capital is crucial to building a successful school. Your teachers play a role in the success or lack thereof and the performance of your school. As you begin building your WIN-time system, here are a few topics to consider before your launch:

1. Do your teachers know how and what to do during small group instruction?

2. Can your teachers analyze data to determine the best interventions and take immediate and swift action?

3. Do your teachers know the expectations of WIN time? Explain what WIN time is and what it is not.

WHAT

What do we use to determine what interventions or enrichment is needed?

Teachers have the ability to use classroom performance on daily work and assessments, universal screeners, and progress monitoring data tools to determine the best interventions and enrichment services to provide. Regardless of the tools used, the determination is based on data, not on how we feel. We use the assessments to determine which students are making progress as expected. Study plans are created for each student performing below grade level, on grade level, and above grade level. A study plan is a checklist of the state standards that are needed to be mastered for each student. As the data is unique for each student, so is the study plan. Interventions for lower-performing students and enrichment for higher-performing students are high-quality, researched-based practices matched to the students' needs. Students above grade-level standards are accelerated at an individual pace specific to the student. Data decisions are essential for an effective WIN-time system.

What assessments do we use and how often do we assess?

Currently, we are using these tools to get baseline data at the beginning, middle, and end of the year on our youngest learners in pre-kindergarten through second grade.

1. **The Primary Reading Inventory (TPRI™)**
   a. Beginning, middle, and end of the year

2. **Developmental Reading Assessment** (DRA) used to determine student reading levels
   a. Beginning, middle, and end of the year
   b. Ongoing to check for growth

3. **Renaissance Reading and Math** used as a screener and a progress monitoring tool throughout the year
   a. Beginning, middle, and end of the year

    b.   Every three weeks for progress monitoring; two-week direct-teach schedule; third-week assessment

For grades 3 and up:

1. **Renaissance Reading and Math**

    a.   Beginning, middle, and end of the year

    b.   Every three weeks for progress monitoring with two weeks of direct teach schedule; on the third week, we assess.

2. **Content-Based Assessments** also known as curriculum-based assessments (CBAs)

    a.   At the end of every grading period

3. **State Assessments**

    a.   State assessments have lag measures to determine if you achieved your goal, but they are hard to correct since the performance has already passed. However, we do look at this data in a longitudinal format, which means we want to see a historical correlation from previous state assessments. Hopefully, we can determine areas of deficiencies that we can intervene on and create a rapid response team on these students before their next state assessment.

What does the schedule look like?

Structure: WIN time is 5 days a week with 2 thirty-minute sessions. We have 3 classroom teachers per grade level. We have self-contained classrooms in pre-k through second grade, and we are departmentalized in grades three and up.

STRUCTURE OF WIN TIME									
Class/ Teacher 1	Class/ Teacher 2	Class/ Teacher 3	Reading Intervention and Dyslexia Specialist	Reading Intervention	Math Intervention	Computer Lab 1 Reading Focus	Computer Lab 2 Math Focus	Special Education	Gifted and Talented or Enrichment
GROUP SIZE									
Group size 1:3 or 1:5	Group size 1:3 or 1:5	Group size 1:3 or 1:5	Group size 1:3 or 1:5	Group size 1:3 or 1:5	Group size 1:3 or 1:5	Group size up to 20	Group size up to 20	Group size 1:3 or 1:5	Group size 1:10
INSTRUCTIONAL MATERIALS AND RESOURCES									
Guided reading, highly-effective, researched-based practices	Guided reading, highly-effective, researched-based practices	Guided reading, highly-effective, researched-based practices	Guided reading, highly-effective, researched-based practices	Read Naturally Program	Highly-effective researched-based practices	Software programs such as IXL or Education Galaxy	Software programs such as IXL, Education Galaxy, and Reflex Math	Highly-effective researched-based practices	Highly-effective researched-based practices

Regardless of your campus size, this can be achieved. As I mentioned previously, I had 10 teachers in each grade level in the district prior to my current principalship. In such a case, I had classroom 1-5 and 6-10 in two different schedules. I also did not have two computer labs available to me in my previous district. Until this WIN time was developed at HES, the two computer labs were not fully utilized. Instead, they were used as an extra location on campus for research and inquiry-type assignments. My hope is for you to look at all the locations on your campus and at the resources you have available to develop a WIN time that is specific to you and your needs.

Example of third grade WIN time: 8:10-8:40 and 8:40-9:10

WHEN

When do groups change?

As a general rule, students stay in their WIN time group for about six weeks. If we progress monitor every third week, the data will showcase the student's growth in at least two checkpoints. Sustainability of the data growth is crucial. We certainly don't want to pull the support if the student is making gains and then have the student take a slide as soon as the support is changed. In some cases, the students make a change after 9 weeks. The need to regroup is based on a student-by-student basis. However, data meetings are held throughout the year to regroup and to replan a large mass of changes.

Learner-centered teaching contains explicit skill instruction.

Let me not confuse you with the textbook definition of explicit teaching as creating and designing lessons that encompass all the parts of a lesson. In the grand scheme of things, this cannot be overlooked. What I'm referencing in this section is matching critical skills to a sequence of content. As we match instructional levels and the selection of appropriately matched curriculum and materials to the students' levels and their abilities, we will ensure high academic success. Based on the students' responses to this instruction, the interventions or enrichments are changed or modified as needed.

Learner-centered instruction embraces students knowing their data and encourages students to reflect on what they are able to know and do.

One of the best interventions is students knowing their own data. We have created data folders for our students to track assessments such as guided reading levels, basic math facts, and their growth on content-based assessments. Even our youngest students track their number and letter identification. After student data is printed and reviewed by the teacher, individual reports are printed for each student. Students have an opportunity to conference with teachers individually to receive words of encouragement and to reflect on their growth from the previous assessment. This small process of creating data folders allows students to take greater ownership of their learning. Our next step is to begin student-led parent-student conferences regarding their data. To get students to embrace the knowledge of their data doesn't happen overnight. This is something that has developed over the last couple of years. The results are worth the efforts of the students and of the teachers who monitor and implement the process.

WHEN

When do groups change?

As a general rule, students stay in the WIN time group for about six-nine weeks. If we progress monitor every third week, the data will showcase the student's growth at least two checkpoints. Sustainability of the data growth is crucial. We certainly don't want to pull the support and then the student takes a slide as soon as the support is changed. In some cases, the students will change after 9 weeks. The need to regroup is based on a student-by-student basis. However, data meetings are held throughout the year to regroup and replan a large mass of changes.

When do we have data meetings and what do they look like?

Data meetings are held at least every 9 weeks. Each teacher or team of teachers meet together to shift instructional groups. Team meetings are held on Wednesdays during PLC time for two reasons. First, teachers are accustomed to planning with the principal on Wednesdays. Second, we progress monitor on Mondays and Tuesdays, so on Wednesdays, the data is ready to be printed and verified. In the meeting, we have in attendance the teachers, the reading and math interventionists, the assistant principal, and me (the principal). Each group of teachers comes in during their conference time and discusses their data and the changes they want to make. Each grade level must come together so the data is reviewed as a grade level instead of as an individual teacher. We do this because as we place students in intervention classes, we are limited on group sizes. If we only have one reading and one math intervention classroom, we must consider placing the lowest-performing students across the grade level.

WHERE

Where do our students go for intervention and enrichment?

As I began my principal position at HES, I audited what instructional materials and interventions were already in place. I was able to draw conclusions that noted our computer labs were underutilized and our intervention classrooms were functioning more as content mastery classrooms, which meant they were available when teachers wanted to send students for extra help. I felt, as most of the staff did, that we had an opportunity to make the most of intervention time. I knew I wanted to change something immediately: students leaving the classroom during instructional time for intervention. This system was only creating more achievement gaps and creating frustration with students who were farther behind when they returned to the classroom after missing the core lesson.

WIN OFFERINGS

1. Reading Lab One focuses on students identified with dyslexia and other reading disorders.
2. Reading Lab Two incorporates Read Naturally™ software to build fluency and comprehension.
3. Our Math Lab focuses on research-based instructional practices and collaborates with the classroom teacher through shared lesson plans.
4. Computer Lab One uses reading programs to support students with their study plans.
5. Computer Lab Two uses math programs to support students with their study plans.
6. Special Education classroom helps support students with an IEP for specialized services.
7. Classroom teachers serve students with guided reading or research-based instructional practices in core subjects.

OTHER WIN OFFERINGS

Are you seeking other ideas? Let me share a few classes for you to consider implementing during WIN time:

1. Science Review

2. Writing intervention

3. STEM/STEAM

4. Robotics

5. Book Club

6. AP Test Prep

7. Study Hall

HOW TO DEVELOP A WIN SYSTEM AT A SECONDARY LEVEL

We understand creating a WIN system at the secondary and middle school levels is different from those at an elementary school level. We know implementing a WIN system is complex. A master schedule and creating an instructional plan for students has to take into consideration the students' credits to graduate, their involvement with extracurricular activities that impact a before- or after-school implementation, not to mention college coursework and the countless social activities. If you are a leader of a secondary school, you may have created an amazing RTI system or you are here seeking suggestions and ideas to overcome some basic challenges. In the next few minutes, we hope to give you some things to brainstorm and things to ponder as you venture down the road of RTI in your secondary school. Keep in mind that there may be aspects that do not perfectly match with your school specifics or align with your personnel resources or your instructional resources.

With that being said, we want to share a few successful methods to consider when creating a master schedule for a middle or high school.

Let me preface my list by saying the best intervention is prevention.
Creating strong intervention and prevention systems in the lower grades
can positively impact secondary campuses. We can't be so naive as to
think this will close the gaps in our students' education. There are many
external factors in play that the school has no control over, such as
student mobility, poverty, homelessness, exposure to drugs and physical
abuse, and even health factors such as stress and anxiety and prolonged
trauma. These factors influence the academic performance of the
students. However, we do have control over many other factors that do
positively affect our students. As a school system, we must create
stronger systems within our walls that make closing the gaps a district
priority. When we create a culture of support and best practices, our
students win. It is imperative that we also implement pacing guides,
create grade-level rigorous instruction that focuses on best practices,
shift our actions from reaction to prevention, and provide positive
behavior supports for engaging students in and out of the classroom.
Even our best interventions cannot adequately achieve success if our
core instructional practices are ineffective.

PLANNING RTI IN SECONDARY SCHOOLS

A list of things to consider:
1.   The best way to achieve a WIN system is to implement it into
     the student's schedule. This requires the student to attend.

2. A and B week/day rotation; example: A week focuses on ELA and B week focuses on math.

3. Add additional minutes to the day creating a WIN time for core subjects such as ELA, math, science, and social studies.

4. Create a homeroom 1st-period allowing students to receive assistance (25-30 minutes).

5. Have instructional specialists available to support classroom teachers inside the classrooms.

6. Implement a co-teaching model allowing two teachers to share the classroom so teachers can work with a group of students.

7. Offer reading or math classes that count as electives; double block students struggling in reading or math. This allows them to receive one core credit and one elective credit.

8. Build a master schedule that allows students to take one class every day for one semester, or take one class every other day for a full year, or take one class every other day for a semester.

YOUR UNIQUE SPIN

There is not just one way to design a master schedule or to provide interventions and enrichments. Your design to implementing this system is unique to your school, your staff, and the students you serve. For the system in your school to work, you must be inspired to put the process in action. If you do not have any parts in place, start by knowing where you are and what are your biggest needs. Most school leaders can determine where they want to be, but they are unsure of where they are at this very minute.

Responding to students through intervention or instruction is a *verb*. It is not a program or a checklist. It is a prevention-oriented approach designed to maximize student achievement.

CRITICAL BELIEFS FOR RTI TO BE SUCCESSFUL

1. It is critical that educators believe all students can learn and that all educators will take responsibility for the learners in their classrooms.

2. It is critical for teachers to teach and to check whether or not students are learning. All assessments become tools for understanding how best to support students.

3. RTI is not an autopsy approach, which means we want to see how students do before we intervene. Instead, be proactive by preventing student failures.

4. RTI is collaborative, and school-wide communication is essential.

5. No intervention programs can compensate for ineffective core instructional practices. Our core classes must have high-quality, research-based instruction that implements a guaranteed and viable curriculum.

PROBLEM OF PRACTICE

This POP centers around *what I need* to create a response-to-intervention system. Our problem of practice is included to give you an example and to spark a thought that will lead to an action on your part. In the back of the book, you will find pages to outline your problem of practice in your school. Use our example as a catalyst or brainstorm with your team to identify a problem on your campus to focus on. Remember, focus on two to three important things and generate a team to help in this effort. Your problem of practice may take a few weeks or a few months, but most importantly, outline the problem and practice an actionable plan with your team to transform your school for a WIN!

One-size-fits-all classrooms

Achievement data indicates our students are below state standards. Intervention classrooms are functioning on a "soft serve" method, which means students attend if or when it is necessary. Intervention services are not scheduled on a consistent or daily basis. The students who do attend are pulled during core instruction time. When students return to class, they are behind and have missed valuable instruction. Teachers are trained on how to differentiate instruction, but the training leaves teachers not confident in the practice. Therefore, classrooms function in a one-size-fits-all instruction and not everyone fits that mold.

Focus Questions:

How can the campus create instructional changes aimed at targeting individual students who are struggling below grade level?

How can the campus create instructional changes aimed at targeting individual students who are excelling above grade level?

How can we prioritize our classroom time to incorporate small group instruction?

What overall purposes are being served currently?

Whose needs are being met?

CHAPTER 8

BUILD YOUR TEAM FOR THE WIN

by *Morris*

"Individual commitment to a group effort – that is what makes
a team work, a company work, a society work, a civilization work.
Perfection is not attainable, but if we chase perfection, we can
catch excellence." Vince Lombardi

One week after being named the lone finalist for my new position at Hawkins ISD, one of my board members asked to have a meeting with me. He wanted to come out to my house so we could have a private conversation. I barely knew him, and I wasn't sure what to expect, but I did know that he was one of the board members who originally voted against me as the lone finalist. I knew from the interviews that we had similar ideas, but I needed to show him that I did want what was best for the school and that I wanted us to WIN!

Needless to say, I was a little on edge, and I was curious about the direction the conversation would go. I could tell he was a businessman who liked things in order and systemic. I did have "home base" on my side, so I thought at least I had that advantage. So the time came, and I was ready to plead my case for the best effort toward a quality school. My wife and I welcomed him into our home, and we moved our conversation to the back porch. It was at this moment that he asked me, "There are over one thousand school districts in the State of Texas. As far as I know, every one of them hands out the same piece of paper at graduation. What can we do to make our district different and our students' experiences memorable for the rest of their lives?"

I sat there for what seemed to be a few minutes contemplating the question. This is really when our journey began. We talked for a few hours about what our ideas were and how we needed a fresh start for the school to announce the unveiling of the new ideas and the new start. We discussed some history and events that had happened. We talked about goals, ideals and what we wanted for our own children. I didn't really know what the first step was, I just knew that I had to take it. I had not even had time to really digest the needs of the district. So, I began listening and asking why. I sought first to understand what had brought this school district to this place and what my role was in its journey.

I truly believe that I was placed in this place for a reason. I had moved closer to my aging parents and had actually purchased a home prior to getting the job before I even knew a job was opening. The school board had a couple of other people they had in mind for the job. I was basically the "compromise"; I was the safe bet and the one they thought would have the experience to lead. There was a split on the board, and I learned the community and the campuses had also experienced this fracture. The crevice ran deep, and I was not fully aware of the depth, but I was about to understand.

KNOWING YOUR TEAM'S STRENGTHS

I inherited a team that had one person who had applied for my job, and others who had less than 3 years' experience between the three of them. These were great people, but they didn't know me. They were loyal to the campus but certainly not to me. There was a distrust in our school that ran higher than usual due to the board fracture. Let me stop here and say that all these people I am mentioning are fine and wonderful people. I do not think they had anything against me, nor did they intentionally try to harm me. I think they had truly been in an environment that had not focused on the team with a common goal. They had a family focus but not a team focus. They had developed a silo environment where everyone went to their places and did their thing. I had one administrator say, "Our last superintendent wanted us to handle things so they did not make it to him. Mr. Lyon wants us to be an instructional leader, and I am not used to that." This is true. My idea and my vision for the district was different. This didn't make the last person before me wrong, it was just different and that required some adjustments.

We spent the first few weeks going through a book study on Carol Dweck's *Growth Mindset* and talking about the difference between a person's performance and their personal being. We had to talk about how we unlink the conversations about performance and the person by using data and ideas of improvement for all. Just because we need to coach someone and help them to be stronger doesn't mean we are saying they are a bad person. This culture of the school had linked a person's performance with who they were as a person, and that had been sewn in them. If a leader had an issue with performance or a deficiency in need of correction and they offered suggestions, then in the staff's mind, it made them a bad person. This by no means was the intention; we just wanted a WIN for those staff members and the kids. We weren't trying to say someone was a bad person because they had not been offered training or resources to build their capacity to teach and learn. This is where we began the conversations and why learners expanded to more than just students. We, as professionals, also had to have an environment and culture of learning. How can anyone think they have arrived, especially when we live in an environment when information doubles exponentially? Even adults must be learner-centered!

Evaluating your team's strengths is essential. Whether you do Myers-Briggs type assessments or Strength Finder, there is power in knowing your team's strengths and weaknesses and how to mesh those skills together so you can complement one another. There are times when your hiring practices should seek a certain strength that your team may be missing. In our transformation course, we have activities that will help you to understand your team's personality and tendencies. This is helpful not only for your immediate team but also for building capacity in your campus teams. It takes different people and different skill sets to help get the WIN! For instance, on a football team, you have linemen who are in the trenches, and the quarterback who executes the plays. It takes a combined effort to achieve the WIN.

ASSEMBLING A WINNING TEAM

If you type the question into your search engine, "What is the single greatest impact on a student's learning?" you will get numerous results on the impact of an effective teacher on a child's educational experience. I expected this result. We all remember those teachers in our life who made a huge impact; we also remember some of the really ineffective ones. This is why it is so important to spend time on recruiting and hiring high-quality people. If you hire a quality person, then you can teach them the direction of your district or school. But if you hire someone to fill a spot, then you are getting what you seek: a place holder.

We have spent a great deal of time revamping our recruiting and onboarding procedures. It is important for our administrators to find quality individuals, and once we do, we want to make a great impression. As we all know, we only have one chance to make a great first impression. I think this is important to consider with new staff. This is a great way to model your expectations and set a great example right from the start. Of course, with our recruiting efforts, we use social media, the Educational Service Center job board and attendance in our local college career fairs but we also go out and try to recruit highly effective people from other districts.

If I was going to answer my board member's question about how we were going to be different, I was going to have to add more high-quality people to our district. I had to bring in the best of the best to try to have a unique educational experience for our students beyond that piece of paper that every other district in the state passes out. No pressure.

So, as I had a position come available for various reasons, we began to search. I have always thought through my experience that if I have a person with a caring heart for students, who has a strong work ethic and has integrity, then I can help point them in the right direction. These are the traits we look for in our staff. If you haven't ever thought about that, I would encourage you to reflect on the type of employee traits you want in your staff.

One of the first hires we had to make was a high school principal. We opened it up, but I had an idea of what we were looking for in a principal. I approached a principal from a neighboring school and asked them to apply if they were interested. This was a person who had ties to the community, and I thought they would be what we needed for our school. We went through the process and the committee landed on her for the recommendation; she had success and our staff respected her.

The power of a network is nothing to underestimate. This new principal had people she had worked with at other districts whom she encouraged to apply as other jobs came available. As we went through our hiring season, we were able to add some great administrators, including Stephanie. Our team was together, and we were headed off to a great start. It was not always a WIN at first; there were times I was told no, or that we didn't get the one that I really thought would be the best for the job on board for various reasons. Let me say, we always have a committee hiring process. I have the final authority to recommend, but I heavily rely on the hiring committee's recommendations. Most of the time our thoughts align, but occasionally, we have a split committee, and I have to make the final call. I feel like when we have a team approach to the hiring process, in most cases, the best candidate will rise to the top.

I have had restarts, where we hired a person and they did not turn out to be what we thought. This will happen from time to time as we all know. I had one teacher that I recruited for a couple of years to apply for a job. I was persistent because just like a coach wants the best players for his team, I want the best for my team. I want the best for my students. Finally, either through me wearing this person down or because the right time came along, we got him on board, and he has been a great asset to our staff. He has brought new life to our ag department and has even had a large part in getting us national recognition recently on *The Today Show*. I guarantee that being on *The Today Show*, live from your school, will make a memorable experience for all involved. Do not ever give up on bringing the best people into your district.

HOW TO KEEP YOUR TEAM FOCUSED - A RALLY CRY

One of the things that my board member and I talked about on that night on my back porch was a rebranding, and I knew we had to have a rally cry. We needed a motto or a slogan for our staff to recognize when we had a moment that required focus or when we wanted to celebrate a victory. This came from discussions in our visioning work as we started working on our new direction. There were many conversations around how academics, extracurricular and athletics all played in the students' educational journey. So, from those discussions, "Game on" was established. I know it is a somewhat simple motto, but at the time it was created, it was a rally cry to bring everyone together and to keep focused on what we were doing. If we had a challenge, then *Game on!* If we had a celebration, then *Game on!* My wife and I had used this approach at other districts, so I knew its value.

We also try to keep the focus on our staff and community through various district communications. Once we had our vision, mission and values established, we put them in a format and had the sign posted throughout the district. We used a publication that highlighted different components of the district at our recruitment fairs and community events. You may be thinking, *well, that's nothing new...large schools do that all the time.* Well, are you using this strategy? Not your district, but you at your campus? Are you fully using every opportunity to communicate and sell your school? If you are doing these things, then what can you do to take it to the next level? What can you do to make your school stand apart? This communication takes on multiple benefits. It keeps your staff speaking the same language, and it keeps them focused. It also sells your brand to the community, so they are supportive. This communication let's other teachers and educational professionals in other districts notice your school, and it might open up your hiring choice for quality candidates.

One final thought in regard to keeping your team focused: it is wonderful when you have a great team assembled. When you feel that synergy and you know you are all firing on all cylinders. There are just a few times in my career when I have felt that feeling. When this happens, success happens. It is just like sports teams or any other great combination of people doing good work. It has never failed that when this happen, people begin to get other opportunities and doors open. I have had a number of quality principals go on to get superintendent jobs or great teachers who have had the opportunity to become principals. That is the goal, and I love it when students and staff reach their goals. As an administrator, I get excited when I see a staff member set a goal and achieve it! It is special when you are able to help people achieve great things, and it is special when you have people working together to achieve for others. Sometimes, staff advancing to their goals will cause a setback in your organization, but you have to have a good "next person up" strategy or keep benefits in place for retention. We are currently looking at ways we can help to retain our amazing staff. We want to continue to provide the best for our students, and we are blessed to have an outstanding staff at our school.

In summary, my answer to our board member about how to make our school stand out more than the other thousand districts that hand out the same piece of paper: people. Our people and their commitment to the children is the key. In order to get the right people, you have to search, you have to recruit, and you have to retain. Keep your people focused through leadership, communication, and caring for them. I am not perfect, and I have fallen short on many things during my leadership journey, but I value our people and I think we have an amazing staff who wants to help kids. We try our best to set up systems to help strengthen our team and to make us all better, but I truly attribute all the success of our school to the quality people we have in place.

PROBLEM OF PRACTICE

This POP centers around *what I need* to build a winning team. Our problem of practice is included to give you an example and to spark a thought that will lead to an action on your part. In the back of the book are pages for you to outline your problem of practice in your school. So, use our example as a catalyst or brainstorm with your team and identify a problem on your campus to focus on. Remember, focus on two to three important things and generate a team to help in this effort. Your problem of practice may take a few weeks or a few months, but most importantly, outline the problem and practice an actionable plan with your team to transform your school for a WIN!

> ### Building an All-Star Team
>
> The principal is new to a school, and there is an opening in a core administrative position. The principal is not sure what the strengths of the core team are, but she wants to build on the strengths and hire someone who compliments the team. She can see that a large portion of the team is new to their positions and still are growing into the roles. Being new to the district, she is not up to speed on the historical influences that have shaped the school. There is one team member who has

been in leadership in the district for many years and has the mentality that things are not broken. However, the data is indicating that some instructional practices need to be implemented. The teachers have had numerous leadership changes over the last four years and are not convinced that the administrative team is dependable.

Focus Questions:

What are the factors to consider?

How can the principal assess strengths to ensure a complementary hire is achieved?

How can the principal lead to a common goal?

What can help build capacity in the team?

What steps should the team take to model a unified front?

How will the principal win the respect of the seasoned admin in the district while implementing a new direction?

How can trust and respect be rebuilt with the teaching staff?

How does the principal mentor the young administrators while balancing all the needs of building teamwork?

How can the principal leverage the strengths of her team to conquer the scenario?

CHAPTER 9

STRUGGLING FOR THE WIN

by *Morris*

"Many of life's failures are people who did not realize how close they were to success when they gave up." Thomas Edison

BE THE MODEL- STAY POSITIVE, STAY CALM

Mindset is everything. This has been more a part of the conversation as we move toward a better understanding of social-emotional learning. This is a key part of an administrator's success. I know it is easy to say but sometimes hard to practice, especially when the pressure is squeezing, and you feel like you have been pushed to your limit or you are tired but continue pushing and working hard to achieve your goals. We all know how this feels; we have all been there. I have learned how to handle this better through experience, but early in my career, I exploded a few times, showing my immaturity. The calmer you stay, the more control of the situation you

111

retain. After all, what kind of example are you showing when you blow up in front of your coworkers? Not a good one.

We see those charismatic leaders who continue to look calm even when the world seems to be coming apart around them. I often think about what they are really thinking on the inside. If you are one who is quick to push the panic button, how do you think the ones who look up to you are feeling? People look to a leader as the one with all the answers when things are tough. If the leader is panicked, it can cause some organizational consequences. Think of a duck swimming across a calm, still, pond in the woods. It may appear that this duck is calm and graceful, but under the water, the duck is paddling like crazy just to stay afloat. Isn't this the picture of a day in the life of an administrator?

The charismatic leader is also one who stays positive. It is so draining when you have those people who are constantly negative or who always have a problem. It is so tiring! Being a positive ambassador for your school and for your campus is crucial, especially in today's landscape of school choice. People want to hear the positives about your school. It doesn't matter if you are public, private, charter or whatever—we have to take on a more customer-service-centered approach in our school and through the story told of our school. We are here to serve, and we are here to make sure that students are getting the best of the best. We must expect this from our staff and model it every day.

I think the most important thing I have learned in my twenty years of being a campus and district leader, is that you have to find balance. You have to know where your limit is and not push past it. There has to be a balance between your professional life and your personal life. I know this is common knowledge; however, we can easily find ourselves breaking this rule. There have to be boundaries set, and you have to be intentional. If you find yourself struggling, then schedule time in for your family or for a day of relaxation. Believe it or not, when you are rested, you think more clearly and often produce higher quality work. I know it is hard to take downtime when deadlines and pressures are mounting, but sometimes, you have to take action and set that boundary for your kids, your spouse and for yourself.

MODEL WHAT YOU WANT TO ACHIEVE

In order to model what you want to achieve and to know where you are heading, you must do some self-reflecting. If you do not have a true compass of your own heading, you sure can't be the guide for others. I know you have had similar conversations, and I just had someone say this in my office earlier today, "Well, ole so-and-so was not happy at her old school, and now she is not happy at her new school. At some point, she has to look at herself to see if it is the school or herself." Don't be ole so-and-so. Make sure you have a good look at yourself and understand your strengths and weaknesses. Do not let those weaknesses be a stumbling block for your life. The first part of fixing a problem is to understand that there is a problem and what it encompasses. There are a lot of great things out there to help you with self-reflection. I have really valued the Strengths Finder 2.0 at https://www.gallup.com/cliftonstrengths/. It was spot on for me, and it has really helped me to understand where my limits are; it has also shown me who I need on my team to make the team stronger. If you really want some deep reflection, look into a self-reflection with 360-degree feedback. This will really bring you to a deep understanding of your tendencies and habits of leadership. This self-reflection is just as it sounds: you choose several of your coworkers to fill out evaluation sheets about you, and it is processed through the assessment tool to help give you some constructive feedback. Feedback from those who work around you on a daily basis can keep you grounded. I believe this tool is most effective when you have been in an organization for more than 18 months.

Once you have built strength within, you must build strength in your staff. A few months ago, I received one of the greatest compliments ever. I had one of the assistant principals in my district tell a group in an administration meeting, "Mr. Lyon builds capacity within the staff, just as he expects us to do in our students. He wants the staff to learn and excel just as much as the students." Man, that will get your batteries charged right there! I was blown away by his statement. You have to be the influence, the model, the one who takes a minute to make a difference or spare a caring moment of encouragement to push someone or to pull them along when they are in a tough spot. You never know what a moment of your time will grow into in a person.

If you expect a strong work ethic and you expect people to work hard for kids, then work hard for them and show your work ethic. Nothing infuriates me more than the old saying, "Do as I say, not as I do." I used to hear that as a kid; it made me mad then, and it makes me mad today. That saying is selfish, narrow-minded nonsense. It should be, "Do as I do, not as I say." Be the model and be the one who leads by example. I am always proud of my principals when they teach a lesson when we can't find a substitute or when they hold a tutorial session for our students. This is a great way to model and lead for their campus. When people see your heart and see that you care, it is magical.

KEEP FOCUSED

One of the first things we did when I came to Hawkins was to do a book study with my administrators. I had just been introduced to Carol Dweck's work on the growth mindset, and I was very interested in introducing that into our school. We assigned chapters and worked through the book and had some great conversations. We have engrained some of this logic into our culture to try to help with staff and students' mindsets. One has to have this mentality with some of the work we do in the education world. We must try what works and not be afraid when it doesn't. We must do what it takes for what our kids need and to help them grow. We have to decide what the most important thing is, and then focus on that in our school. As stated in Chapter 3, our focus was on being learner-centered. We wanted to make sure we were putting our efforts towards that vision.

I recently did a school board training with a great group of board members. They were frustrated over the lack of support for a local bond issue for school facility improvements. We worked on a conversation tool that helped to pull out the why in their reasoning for proposing another bond issue. We prioritized the comments and put together a list of talking points to come back to in their conversations in their communities. We discussed several strategies. They truly want what is best for the school but were frustrated with the failure of the last several bond issues. Their past elections had gone in different planning directions from what their original intent was meant to be. They had been concerned about school safety, but due to a lack of focus, they had begun to include athletic improvements and other items in the list of needed improvements. I think they also lost focus as a board and had presented a mixed message to the community. Stephanie and I do a lot of this work with visioning and trying to get school values, ideas, strategies and a vision all in line with a common vocabulary. This is what I tried to do with this board's idea for facilities. I left that night with a good feeling that our training had the board getting back in the core of their beliefs about the main reason for calling a bond issue. I hope they are successful in their next attempt.

We can easily get knocked off of center in many things we do in our organization, work, or personal life. We must have our core set of beliefs that we hold tight to and center ourselves to those beliefs. It is good to have those beliefs posted so we can see them often and help to remind ourselves if we start to stray away from what is most important.

WIN THE WAR

Sometimes, "you can't see the forest for the trees." So many times we get sidetracked on the little things, and we cannot see the big picture. This parallels to keeping the focus. Winning the war is about keeping the important thing the important thing. We have to know when to hold tight and when to relax. So often, especially when we first start as out as an administrator, we want to make sure we win every single issue. It is like a giant scoreboard floating in the air, following us around with tally marks on it. Here are some words of wisdom that I wish I had early on: *You're not going to win every battle. Why would you want to invest the energy in winning every little battle? When it comes to a strategic plan of warfare, there is a thing called strategy.*

I have seen some administrators spend a tremendous amount of time on things that do not matter! Why would someone spend hours designing and scaling out a parking lot diagram because some teacher complained about losing her self-proclaimed parking spot? Does the administrator feel the need to map out a detailed plotting map to try to keep the peace? I have seen people chase down a stapler for hours, costing staff time and resources beyond the cost of the stapler that was being hunted. We get lost amongst the trees and we can't see the big picture or exercise good practice because we are too close to the issue; perhaps we have an emotional connection interwoven into the situation. These are examples of people not keeping their focus on the important work of helping kids. They get caught up in winning a battle that is not worth fighting.

As administrators, we must have the judgment and understanding of what is worth our time. I am not saying to brush off your community member who has an issue and wants to talk about something you think is not worth your time. However, I am saying you can frame that conversation in a way to focus it on the important things, lend a listening ear, and move to a resolution to help get you in a position to help the outcome. Keep your focus on what is important to your campus when working through the day and in the decisions you make. Make sure you stay centered in this thought, and do not get caught up in trying to win the battles that do not support the main thing.

HOW DOES YOUR CAMERA LENS SEE THE WORLD?

My youngest daughter recently purchased a new camera with her own money! This is a big deal; she is in sixth grade. This camera is nicer than any I have owned; it cost her $400. It has a zoom lens and different settings, so it is pretty fancy. I am quite content with the camera on my cell phone; I think it takes pretty good pictures for what it is. My girls often hate to have pictures taken with my wife's phone; they say it doesn't take clear enough pictures for them. We have a tradition of each summer going on family trips with the vision or big goal of getting them to all 50 states by the time they graduate. So, this picture-taking thing is important so we can capture those moments of us traveling together.

I think this example plays a part in times when we struggle as administrators. We are looking through our camera lens and not considering the picture that is being captured by those around us. We all have different cameras we are looking through. We may have those around us with the big expensive zoom lens that can take a picture from a mile away, or we have those with a small, inexpensive camera who struggle just to get a clear shot. We have those who have a camera that is carried in a nice case and housed in a plush environment where no bad things are ever encountered, and we have those with cameras that have been dropped and broken but still manage to take a picture. We have those who have the old vintage cameras with the flashbulbs that rotate and may not adapt well to the latest technology, and we have those who will buy the latest and greatest even though they purchased a new camera just six months ago. Often, we are so worried about our focus and perfect shot that we forget about the vantage point of others around us.

Just think how powerful our schools would be if everyone took a minute to consider what other vantage points are around us and how the same picture is being seen before we take the shot. Think about how much clearer a picture could be with everyone's input and listening to how the focal point looks through their lenses. This would truly ensure that the best picture was taken of the subject. While we aspire to do this, I believe there are times when we don't. There are times when we rush through an important decision without the consideration of others. We do not always take the educational differences, cultural differences or economic differences in to play when we make a decision that impacts all our children. I urge you, before you take that next shot, pause for a moment and see what it looks like through someone else's lens.

In summary, if you are struggling, make sure you take time and recharge your batteries, so you are able to focus on the important things. We have to keep the big things the big things and work on the correct work. Don't burn your energy on things that are not going to have the right impact. Stay calm and stay focused on the war, not on winning every battle. Most importantly, keep others in mind and take the time to consider how your decisions will impact others. Often, if you take time to see other points of view, it might save you time and energy in making your idea, initiative, or project even better before you introduce it. Be your best self, follow your heart, be grateful, be courteous, and continue to learn, listen, lead, and never give up!

PROBLEM OF PRACTICE

This POP centers around *what I need* to create a new focus for your school. Our problem of practice is included to give you an example and to spark a thought that will lead to an action on your part. In the back of the book are pages for you to outline your problem of practice in your school. So, use our example as a catalyst or brainstorm with your team and identify a problem on your campus to focus on. Remember, focus on two to three important things and generate a team to help in this effort. Your problem of practice may take a few weeks or a few months, but most importantly, outline the problem and practice an actionable plan with your team to transform your school for a WIN!

Overcoming the Struggle

A principal is in his sixth year as an administrator. He feels he has learned a great deal from his active mentor and through some bumps and scrapes experienced on his campus. For the past few years, he has been on his game, and the campus has experienced some awards and accolades for academic success. However, due to some recent changes from the state education agency toward the accountability system, a child entering into college, aging parents that are requiring more time, and some health problems with his spouse, the world is closing in and stresses are pouring in. The principal is having to take family members to doctor appointments so the number of work days missed is piling up and things are starting to slip. The superintendent has noticed some rumblings by teachers and some issues with discipline on the campus and has sent his concerns to the principal. The emotional and physical toll is crushing the principal's determination and energy to control his world.

Focus Questions:

How important is work/life balance?

What boundaries should the principal implement to ensure campus stability?

How could a system help to resolve this problem?

What lens is the superintendent looking through?

How could a unified team help this situation?

What should focus should the principal have during this time?

What should the priorities be in this situation?

How would you react as a leader if this was one of your teachers instead of the principal?

CHAPTER 10

PROFESSIONAL LEARNING COMMUNITY AND THE IMPACT ON STUDENT ACHIEVEMENT

by *Stephanie*

"People are empowered not by that which they know is true but rather that which they believe is possible."- unknown

We can all acknowledge that the fundamental purpose of our school should be to help all students achieve high levels of success. If that statement is correct, we should take a minute and examine our own practices and the impact of our leadership on student performance. At HES, we employ the practice of professional learning communities (PLCs) to design rigorous instruction that will ultimately improve student learning. I don't proclaim to be an expert in the PLC model, but I do know that the model gives us a framework to build teacher capacity and allows us to work as a collaborative team with the notion to improve student learning. Without stating tons of research behind views on PLCs, I will share with you the results from our campus and our glimpses into the process. I tend to enjoy seeing the work in practice. This is practical, and it allows you to take what you need from this chapter and use it right away.

As I share with you the PLC model at my school, keep in mind that it is likely that our PLC may differ from yours and yours from other schools. Regardless of your dynamics, if done well, we improve learner outcomes, teachers will improve instruction by learning from each other, we will create sustainable campus-wide change, and we will have significant value-added to both behavior and academic data.

With the understanding of what PLC is, we should also address what PLC is not. A PLC is not a program, a verb, or a meeting. As my friend Cristi Parsons always says, *it is who we are and what we do.* Keeping the concept or the simple definition in your mind, let me share an example of it at work on my campus. An early career teacher struggles with small group instruction. She struggles to know what the rest of the students should be doing while she is working with a group of students. Fortunately, a veteran teacher on campus has a clear understanding of small group instruction, and her students are learning at grade level or higher on assessments. The veteran teacher models small group instruction while the other teacher observes this in action. The two teachers collaborate and share resources that will keep students engaged so she can focus on the small group lessons. This is an example of a PLC. By focusing on a solution together, the teacher and the campus will see student results faster. After all, increased student achievement is the number one indicator of a successful PLC.

Do you remember the movie *The Pursuit of Happyness*? Let me refresh your memory if you haven't watched it or if it has been a long time since you did. It is based on a true story about a man named Chris Garner, who is played by Will Smith. He is a struggling single father who has been evicted from his apartment. He and his son have no place to go and roam from shelters and public restrooms only to face many more hardships throughout the movie. Chris refuses to give in to despair as he struggles to create a better life for himself and his son.

A very intriguing message of the movie caught my attention when Chris told his son these words: *"You got a dream. You got to protect it. People can't do something themselves; they want to tell you that you can't do it. If you want something, go get it."* I think so many people, including myself, gravitated to the story because it is a message of perseverance, determination, and pure hard work. If we work hard enough and long enough, we can achieve anything.

Why am I telling you a story about one of my favorite movies from 2006, and how does this relate to PLCs?

Here's why:

People are empowered not by that which they know is true but rather that which they believe is possible.

In other words, teachers are not empowered to bring about change simply by numbers in a spreadsheet, steps to take, facts to analyze, and figures in charts and graphs. Instead, we are all driven to make an impact when we have the opportunity to bring greater value to the overall grand scheme of things. When we truly understand what we are doing and how it makes a difference, we can't help but want to be a part of something bigger than just ourselves. This action makes us question what future we hope to create for our school and what each team member must do to fulfill that purpose. There is no more powerful pursuit driving your school toward excellence than a vision for the future. Having a shared vision is essential for the school, but it is also a critical element used to empower your staff to have a clear purpose to rally behind. If the vision of the school is equally aligned to the work of the PLC, our teams will genuinely be strengthened to be a united community of learners.

DEEPENING LEARNING AT HES

Fostering collaboration

Fostering the need for your staff to collaborate isn't just "nice to have"; instead, it is a "must have" strategy that all leaders are beginning to address. If we don't take the time to collaborate with each other, you will struggle to achieve the campus goals.

Why is that true?

When your team doesn't take time to collaborate and work together on a goal or on a task leading to the goal, there will be a lack of alignment. If we don't know what the other team members are doing, how can we be aligned? Second, ineffective communication can be one of the reasons behind failing to meet the goal.

We have all probably experienced working on a team. Knowing how a team works, you can easily recognize a dysfunctional team. These are the kind of teams where one or two individuals micromanage the entire group, or other group members really don't do their fair share of the work. When team members are more concerned about themselves, this can be detrimental to the campus. This kind of teamwork will not just keep the campus from moving forward; it will erode the relationships and make any and all work on the campus difficult.

I was at an educational conference, and I signed up to sit at a roundtable discussion. The morning sessions were in a large conference room, and they functioned like speed dating. We were all given enough time to rotate to at least three tables before going to the next section of the event. The first table I chose was a hot topic because others joined the table. The table host did not show, so all the attendees sat and shared our backgrounds and insights on the topic. It turned out to be a great table discussion regardless of the lack of a table host. Each member of the table stepped forward and exchanged conversations about what was working and what wasn't on our campuses. It wasn't until the third table where my eyes as an administrator were opened. The table host was a principal who shared insights on the given table topic. She began to talk and share resources and ideas. At first, I thought it would be to help spark conversation and for us to collaborate. After all, this was what the entire purpose of the session was to be used for—to collaborate with other leaders.

Instead, when a table member simply shared in response to something the host said, the principal never acknowledged the conversation. This did not happen just once. It happened every single time. Each time it happened, I noticed the table members begin to no longer have anything to say. It reminded me of the quote from Andy Stanley, "Leaders who don't listen will eventually be surrounded by people who have nothing to say." Listening is a powerful skill for leaders.

Understanding the value of fostering collaboration, I make it a point to model this behavior myself. It is important that we encourage collaboration through as many possible opportunities as possible.

One of the biggest factors that contribute to the success of any school is whether we perform as a team.

As the principal, superintendent, or any other school leader, we can give teachers the opportunities to brainstorm on various projects or initiatives such as determining our campus goals, or how we can better utilize our resources, or even building management processes such as our dismissal process or student recognition programs. Collaboration is powerful, not only because it cultivates teamwork and we ultimately achieve our purpose. But collaboration is more than that. Everyone is providing value and voice and creating meaningful work, and we begin to experience a return on our time. There is nothing more amazing than to watch a collective talent work together to problem-solve, discuss, and share project ideas. When this happens, the capacity of each individual member of the campus grows and then equally our students benefit.

Teachers Observing Teachers

Outside the educational setting, observing other professionals is a common practice. We see this in the medical field, professional business, and skilled laborer positions in manufacturing and in skilled trades. In these different positions, it is called job shadowing. Job shadowing allows the new employee to have job training by following a trained and experienced employee. As I reflect on how this practice is used, I think to myself, *why wouldn't this be a strategy that is used in education?* This can be the most effective professional development strategy in which to grow our teachers. I have always said, some of our very best training happens under our very roof every day. We just need to capitalize on the talents in our own building.

I remember the very first time we had a training on instructional strategies. Following my first year at HES, I took my classroom observation data and determined instructional strategies needed to be a focus. We needed to make some improvements in active learning and student engagement. Therefore, we shared a quick overview of several high-impact instructional strategies. The hope was that with practice in these strategies, students, and teachers would be able to select the right strategies at the right time and truly help the students understand the concepts and skills better. As with any training, we had the traditional PowerPoint presentation with discussions of each instructional strategy. Following the session in the training room, we gathered our notepads and walked through several classrooms in the building to spot and document all the various instructional strategies being used. This simple task opened the door by allowing this to now be a common professional learning practice. Teachers stated the learning walk helped them to visually identify the different instructional strategies that had just been discussed in the training room. Another reflective response was that teachers had forgotten about some of the powerful strategies they had used in the past. They quickly jotted them down to begin using again in their classrooms. This simple practice helps to enhance our teaching methods and enriches student learning, and it allows teachers to become reflective about their own teaching skills.

Other opportunities of teachers observing teachers or of teachers collaborating over instruction happens often, but let me share about a time when teachers in kindergarten through second grade shared a guided reading lesson with each other. We were in the middle of a book study using Jan Richardson's book, *The Next Step Forward in Guided Reading.* The book is filled with instructional tools that can be used right away. One tool is specific lesson plan templates for each level of guided reading. I had asked the teachers to read the chapter that aligned to their grade level and to reference the lesson plan template that corresponded with it. Over the next few weeks, the teachers worked on guided reading lessons in small groups within their classrooms. Following the two weeks, we met together after school and discussed the lessons. The teachers shared what worked well and what they needed to improve upon for next time. Teachers gave suggestions and valuable input to one another. Each teacher was at a different stage of small group guided reading experience; some were more experienced, and some were at the beginner level. No matter what level or stage of experience, we all had an opportunity to learn from each other.

Taking the opportunity to capitalize on observing and learning from one another, we were increasing our focus on student achievement. There were various other benefits, such as opportunities to build more confident teachers and an increased sense of campus accountability.

Vertical Alignment: Striving for Success

As much as I saw the need for vertical aligning, the process didn't start right away. The whirlwind took control of my actions in the first few years. I'm not making any excuses other than I had to focus on one or two big goals that would give me the most significant impact on student achievement. For me, the first few years were spent redesigning the intervention system and revamping student engagement to help decrease discipline. I'm excited to see the vertical alignment taking place. We are striving for success in this area. Vertical alignment comes with a few struggles, such as trying to find the time for teachers to collaborate across grade levels. We know getting teachers together before or after school is not feasible, so during the school day, we are working to get all the math teachers or the reading teachers together to discuss their state standards, plan together, or share resources. We are up for the challenge. With all of that in mind, I did some frontloading of the tasks. We began by deconstructing standards. In order for us to dig deep in teaching the standards, we had to determine the standards that were essential, or what we now call our power standards. We all know some standards carry a larger weight because they have a tremendous impact as they are a prerequisite for the next grade level or because they are likely to be a standard that will appear on our state assessment. Each grade level analyzed these standards, which continue to remain in our conference room walls. Each week when we have grade level planning, we read through our standards to understand the specificity of what we want our students to know and be able to do. Devoting time to analyzing our standards paved the way for us to have a vertical alignment session in the first semester and one again in the second semester of the school year. On this vertical alignment day, it was fully teacher-led. Who else better to really discuss their standards than the very teachers who teach it every day? The teachers discussed what each grade level expected their students to know entering the grade level. They modeled how to teach difficult standards, and they discussed best instructional resources that they are finding meaningful and helpful in their classrooms.

We may be farther behind on the vertical alignment journey than other schools. However, we are making great strides every year. All that matters is that we all end up on the other side of the mountain together.

Data Digs

I love data. I'm not going to lie to you or cover up the fact that I can't function without it. Data can lead to some great discoveries. We are inundated with both teacher data and student data. We have to use it to our advantage. I am known for saying this quote all the time: *Data remains data until it is acted upon in intentional ways.* In other words, we must take action on the data.

Recently, we administered an assessment of our younger elementary students. This is common practice at the beginning, middle, and end of the year. During a grade level planning meeting, we took a look at the data and determined areas in which we could improve in the skill before we assessed again at the end of the year. This is just one example of the campus collecting the data, acting upon it, and communicating the results with each other. Data digs is a common practice that happens monthly. In the end, we have a clear and concise picture of where we are and where we need to go. Equally important, we can determine the relationship between the assessment and its connection to student learning and achievement.

Through the use of collaboration, teachers observing one another, vertical alignment and data digs, we are deepening learning for not just our students; teachers are growing in subject matter, curriculum, and teaching practices. It is important to prepare our teachers and students to be successful; if we're not doing that, then we shouldn't exist, in my opinion.

PROBLEM OF PRACTICE

This POP centers around *what I need* to deepen learning at your school.

Our problem of practice is included to give you an example and to spark

a thought that will lead to an action on your part. In the back of the book,

you will find pages to outline your problem of practice in your school.

Use our example as a catalyst or brainstorm with your team to identify a

problem on your campus to focus on. Remember, focus on two to three

important things and generate a team to help in this effort. Your problem

of practice may take a few weeks or a few months, but most importantly,

outline the problem and practice an actionable plan with your team to

transform your school for a WIN!

Increase the rigor of instruction in the classroom; lack of engagement

Classroom observations, student discipline data, and student learning data all indicate the need to change our instructional methods. It is evident that students are not actively engaged in the lessons. Students are off-task because they are not interested, they are not actively involved in the classroom tasks, or the teaching is not connecting the content to the student. There is a need for more instructional strategies that engage students, and there is a need to increase the rigor of instruction to allow students to achieve at higher levels.

Focus Questions:

In classrooms in which data is at or above average, what strategies are these teachers using to engage students?

In classrooms in which data is at or above average, what does more rigorous examples of work look like?

How can we get students to respond positively to more rigorous content?

Are students being given opportunities to actively participate in the lessons or are the classrooms more teacher-driven?

CHAPTER 11

SUSTAINABILITY FOR THE WIN

by *Morris*

"My system of railroading is to take care of it just as careful as
I would of my own household affairs, handle it just as though it
was all mine; and take good care of its income; that is my aim, you
know, and give that to the stockholders." Cornelius Vanderbilt

BUILDING A LEGACY

Cornelius Vanderbilt was one of the great industrial minds of the nineteenth century who built a legacy of wealth and was responsible for structures such as Grand Central Station. Mr. Vanderbilt was born into transportation; his father operated a sailboat. He bought his own sailboat as a young man ,and then went into steam-powered boats and finally the railroad. He was a pioneer in the growth of the transportation industry during the industrial revolution in American history. Cornelius Vanderbilt was not the creator of the sailboat, steamboat or the railroad, but he was an innovator. He was able to take a system already created and make it more relevant for the current times.

The traits of any great leader or innovator is to take the current issues or environment at hand and to make it more productive and more relevant. Vanderbilt helped to refine steam-powered engines so that transportation was more efficient. Vanderbilt also purchased many Civil War era railways and began to link them together to build an interwoven system of transportation that helped to boost the industrial revolution. Had there not been a means of transportation during this time of our nation, the expansion of America and the growth of industry would have been lessened due to the constraints of access to natural resources.

Cornelius Vanderbilt was not only an innovator but also one who understood sustainability. After he had acquired his system of railroads, there was much more competition in the market. He understood that in order for him to continue to make money and to have his trains full of cargo, he must broker a business deal. Many of the ideas and partnerships created by Vanderbilt are commonplace today, but during this time, he was chartering new ground. Vanderbilt reached out to a struggling young oilman named John E Rockefeller and agreed to a transportation deal hauling Rockefeller's oil; in turn, Rockefeller agreed to fill Vanderbilt's trains to ensure a steady and continuous flow of cargo. Vanderbilt, through his innovation and commitment to his business, was at one time the richest man in America, compiling well over a trillion dollars in today's currency.

These times are so synonymous with our education world today, well...except the vast wealth of resources. Like in the days of Cornelius Vanderbilt, I believe education is in the transformation phase. We are currently working alongside people who are making innovations in education. Those who build a sound system that meets the demand of our current environment will create the innovations that lead to new practices. There are many factors that are impacting our educational environment. The affordability of technology integration in the classroom, new ideas of flipped or blended classrooms, charter schools and the push for privatization across the nation. We all know the external factors that are driving our schools; the most pressure is from increased accountability and the technology advancement used in everyday life outside the school walls.

The integration of technology, in my opinion, has the greatest impact on the classroom for unlimited possibilities. For so long, at the turn of the century, we heard about 21st-century schools and the need to create

21st-century learners, but so many are still performing the "sit and get" mentality because that is the way it was taught to them. The true innovators in our current education landscape are those like Vanderbilt who are not afraid to take risks, employ fresh ideas and build partnerships with community partners to benefit the goals of the school. These partnerships allow for training in workforce jobs with current career-focused technologies that must be mastered by our students. How schools partner and tap into the community resources to advance STEAM to provide a problem-of-practice-type learning along with college and career readiness will be the true innovators of the new frontier of education.

As Vanderbilt said, "My system of railroading is to take care of it just as careful as I would of my own household affairs….". This is important to keep in mind; we must know our vision and our goals and focus our efforts on the direction of our school and community. Having worked at different districts, it is important to understand each school's priority and the opportunities available to that school. So, make sure that as you build sustainability, you are building it for the community and not for you personally. This is key to sustainability.

The vision of the leader is so important to build systems for sustainability. This is true as long as that leader is keeping the "household affairs" to what is best for the "household" and not tweaking "household affairs" to what is best for the head of household. A school will flourish when all the stakeholders have input and are offered buy-in. If everyone understands why things are happening, then they will be more likely to support the vision and direction, which will ensure sustainability. Like Vanderbilt, if your stockholders are the community, then it is important that you meet their needs and build a system around the community.

Stakeholder Buy-In = Sustainability

Successful schools that form their vision around the community are implementing systems that make a connection in all areas of the school. This is similar to how Vanderbilt connected the railways and why the transportation route was more efficient and made more sense. This is true with systems in the educational field. I have seen so many schools that have the processes in place for each issue or program, but they do not connect to an efficient transport of knowledge. This system efficiency is discussed in greater detail in Chapter 6.

A sustainability tale of two schools

As stated above, each community and each school is different. I have been at a few different schools, but I want to give an example of how different these schools are and how I learned from my mistakes along the way. As Cornelius Vanderbilt learned, even though we love to win, we can make mistakes along the way. The important thing is to learn from those mistakes and not to make them again. Vanderbilt was taught a valuable lesson by a couple of members of the board of directors with the Erie Railroad who maneuvered him out of several million dollars in today's currency. While at the time, it was not illegal, it did teach Vanderbilt a sense of strategy and awareness.

Just as Vanderbilt learned from mistakes, so have I done when building systems for school districts. This is a tale about two different school districts, and hopefully, this will help to clarify some of the points above about sustainability. We will label the first district in this example Bottleneck ISD and the second district Shared Vision ISD.

Bottleneck ISD has a unique set of needs. Bottleneck ISD had many great dedicated employees who love kids and want what is best for them.

Bottleneck has performed well on state accountability scores, and mastery of the standards is above average for their cohort group. The needs of this district are to improve upon current practices and to try to increase a good district to a great district. Some ideas to do this is to increase the use of technology in the classroom and to implement project-based learning (PBL).

As with many new initiatives, change is hard and pushback is often experienced, especially when all the stakeholders are not completely involved in the vision of the district. PBL was taken with skepticism and uncertainty. Training and a plan of action were rolled out by the administration. Some initial success was seen in the student performance due to some attention to staffing, response to intervention and focus on underperforming subgroups. However, due to lack of buy-in and uncertainty in the new direction, turnover of staff began, and new faculty were introduced into the system. In some ways, this was a benefit due to younger teachers with more technology skills entering the school and providing for advancement in the PBL initiative. However, the lack of a common shared vision and a total buy-in in the new direction, caused unrest and uncertainty. One unseen threat to the district was the limited human resources available to the district. Finding quality replacements began to be a problem. A few administrators were left and forced to drive the direction of the school, and this caused a bottleneck.

When a bottleneck occurs, it slows down the flow of the vessel. So the growth and expansion of the school were slowed due to the lack of ownership in all the employees. This then leads to lack of responsibility or ownership. The direction of the district was on the correct path but when the stakeholders do not have buy-in, sustainability will suffer.

Many schools fell into the technology trap in the early 2000s. The thought was, if we get the technology, then all will be solved. Instead of focusing on the standards and providing opportunities for problem-of-practice situations, the idea was that the use of Web 2.0 tools would help to advance our schools. Those schools that went down that path have now learned that focus should be on the task the students are doing, and the processing of the task using technology is the key.

Bottleneck ISD enjoyed some success during this time and met many milestones in the PBL initiative. However, once the core group of administrators who were leading the direction of the district left, the PBL initiative and the growth in accountability diminished. The lack of involving all the stakeholders caused the systems that were in place to be unsustainable, and it set the district back.

Shared Vision ISD took a different approach but had different needs. Had the leader of Bottleneck ISD implemented the same PBL initiative at Shared Vision ISD, it would have been a total failure. A previously failed implementation of PBL had caused the destruction of trust in the district. The leader of Shared Vision ISD knew there must be a common buy-in and vision in order for the district to move forward over time and not to suffer a setback upon the departure of the current administration. Unlike Bottleneck ISD, the performance on state standards was not average; they were in fact below average. A continuous curriculum plan and a lack of organizational systems were not in place, so upon building a common vision, a four-year plan of action was put into place.

The new plan had a system to encourage reflection and input among the stakeholders. The administration ensured a common voice and continuous input from all the staff to ensure ownership in the school in order to build sustainability. Just like Bottleneck ISD, some turnover began, but there was a better human resource pool to pull from to ensure quality candidates. The work with stakeholders during the vision process produced a larger community support base for the school and the initiatives. Systems were built to ensure a thorough presentation of the state standards through peer accountability and reflection.

As a result of a shared common vision, wins began to happen. Student performance began to rise and extracurricular and athletics began to improve. Numerous awards were received by Shared Vision ISD and nationally recognized partnerships were celebrated. At the conclusion of year four, a systematic school was developed with a team that could easily work and substitute for one another. While both schools had an outstanding administration team with quality individuals, the Shared Vision ISD would not suffer a complete restructure due to the loss of one or two people. Unlike Bottleneck ISD, Shared Vision ISD had shared in the decision process and was intentional in communicating the common vision, goals and the "why" behind the decisions of the district. This common understanding and belief in the system would help to sustain the school as leadership transitions happen. Change would continue to happen, and new partnerships would have to be engaged, just as Vanderbilt partnered with Rockefeller, in order to survive, but the core direction would be instilled, so a setback for students was less likely.

The keys to sustainability:

1) A shared common vision—communicate, communicate, communicate

2) Collaborative leadership—shared decision making

3) Stakeholder buy-in—build for the community

4) Flexibility to the environment—willingness to make changes when needed

5) Solid systems that encourage professional dialogue and growth

DEVELOPING YOUR STAFF VS. STAFF DEVELOPMENT

How do you use your staff development time? Is it well planned and systematic, or is it a last-minute "workday"? I am guilty of many different uses of staff development, not because I am unprepared but because it is important to know your staff and to understand the needs of your campus. One of the traits I believe is essential is to understand the strengths and needs of your teachers and staff. Please do not think I am downplaying the overall need for a staff development plan. We distribute the spring staff development survey to assess the needs of the campus, and our principals do a very good job through PLCs and our reflective practice to keep a pulse on the needs of the campus. I am a huge believer in vision, so there must be an overarching purpose to the staff development plan. Much like the systems we use for student-driven instruction, the professional development plan should be a framework that we follow so our campus principals have the flexibility to meet the goals of individual learners. As we move to fulfill our overall district vision, "To be the model of a learner-centered school," we are moving our staff development to more of an individualized professional staff development than having a one-size-fits-all approach.

Any time we can model our classroom expectations as administrators, the deeper the connection we can make with our staff. After all, don't you like it better when your supervisor walks the walk instead of just talking the talk? Much of our instructional success has come from individualized learning and from developing a system that caters to an individualized format. As outlined earlier in the book, "WIN time" is a systematic process to ensure that we have different opportunities for our student learners to meet their goals. So, if you truly want to be "learner-centered," this should also include the staff. We use PLCs and reflective practice in much of our work, but a truly individualized-based staff development process is our goal. We have made the process toward this model, but we are not there yet. We set individualized goals in our teacher evaluation system, but often this is focused on classroom performance or it gets off-centered from true personal growth. Schools who have instructional coaches use these staff members to help increase capacity in professional growth. But, is it truly individualized? Individualized development of staff is one of our ongoing goals to help with professional growth rather than having staff development sessions. This will be the POP example for this chapter.

When approaching staff development, schools often focus on staff development as meeting the required training from the state and maybe rolling a new program. We continue to do this as well, but we have tried to make it more flexible along with moving toward the more individualized approach. With all our required annual staff development, we use an online platform, which is also available for the teachers during the summer. We have a deadline to have the training done by the first day of school. We have compensatory days built in the school calendar for professional development outside normal contracted days. Also, occasionally we will introduce a new program or a new resource to help our students and staff. We also have built in-service days at the end of the school year so new initiatives are introduced at the beginning of the summer rather than a week before the students return. This allows our staff more time to digest the new initiative and to be better prepared for the new school year. As we all know, anything that we can do to reduce the stress load on teachers right at the beginning of school will help the staff to be more productive and prepared to welcome students back to school.

We have made an effort over the past few years to work on battling these old habits to make our development of staff even better. The flexibility of the required trainings and the introduction of new initiatives is just part of our plan. In order to help with the development of our staff, we have introduced our 3D model of development, which includes delivery of instruction, dialogue and development of staff.

In the 3D model, the first D stands for the delivery of instruction, which focuses on anything around improving our craft of instructional delivery. Under the delivery piece of the 3D model, we focus on our curriculum, lesson planning, vertical alignment, determining our

power standards, data understanding and usage, PLCs, high impact instructional strategies or any other areas that will help improve the delivery of instruction or strengthen our instructional core.

The second D is ensuring a professional dialogue. A professional dialogue is needed to ensure a common understanding. We all have different educational backgrounds and experiences or different cultural and economic differences; a diversified staff can make our staff team very strong, unless professional dialogue is missing. One thing I have learned, unless we are communicating and facilitating a conversation with a common vocabulary, then we may have different understandings of what is expected. I once asked an instructional leader in my district to help deliver professional development to combat our deficiency in differentiated instruction. Having had conversations about RTI and the need for interventions, I made the assumption that when I asked for training to be delivered on differentiated learning, I meant how to reach students at different levels of mastery. My line of thinking was that we needed to have some training on how to set up small group instruction or high impact instructional strategies to give our teachers more tools in their toolbox. It seemed as if the instructional leader and I were on the same page. A couple of weeks later, I stopped by training to see the progress and delivery of professional development. I quickly realized that our ideas of differentiated instruction were not aligned. The training that was being delivered was based on learning styles not differentiated learning. At that moment, I understood the importance of a common academic vocabulary. As a leader, we must ensure that when we set an expectation, it is clear to everyone; never make assumptions because assumptions can waste time and resources. I have learned this the hard way. Now, I often ask to have someone repeat to me what they understand in an assignment, or I will continue to ask questions so that I am confident we are on the same page.

Another valuable tool in the dialogue portion of 3D that is extremely powerful revolves around reflection. Through a reflective process, many of the misunderstandings, as given in the previous example, can be identified. Building in time for reflection is an important tool for an administrator. Reflection is a powerful tool to help improve personal and organizational practices. We have implemented systems that foster accountability but mostly provide for reflective practice. The reflective practice models revolve around the instructional core: the content, the student, the teacher and the task, which is at the center of the instructional core. From these practices of reflection, our administrative team is able to discuss organizational strengths and weaknesses while being immersed in the classroom. This has been not only a powerful tool for our school, but the presence in the classroom has established a new culture on the importance of instruction in our district. The gallery walks have helped to foster professional dialogue and reflection around student work. This tool has given us concrete examples to have good instructional conversations for our teachers with minimal effort in preparation. Do not underestimate the power of reflection.

The third and final D in the 3D model is the development of staff. This is the portion of the 3D model where our district is trying to build in the individualized development of staff. Through evaluations, gallery walks, data from formative and summative assessments, along with instructional round data, we are forming a profile of strengths and areas of refinement. After formulating an electronic portfolio with areas of refinement agreed upon by the teacher and administrator, coaching and development can begin through a targeted approach. Developing a flipped professional development approach while integrating an online professional development platform will help us with our limited instructional coaching staff. We are exploring the possibilities of partnering with neighboring districts and our educational service center to attempt to offer as many individualized opportunities as possible, rather than the "all call sit and get." After all, as discussed earlier, as administrators, we need to encourage and model what we expect in the classroom from our teachers.

Our goal with the 3D model will be to exemplify our vision in the systems we use at the district. Part of the development of the staff should be spent on clarifying the common purpose and vision of the district. If a common vision is created, it must be communicated, and the staff must be aware of the direction of the district. Otherwise, an organization will be pulling in different directions instead of pulling together. We knew we had to build capacity in our teacher leaders and our new staff, so a focus has been made toward mentoring and coaching.

MENTORING AND COACHING

During our planning time this past spring, our administration team realized we had to make mentoring a priority. Sustainability was our main reason for implementing a mentoring program, and in order for the plan to really be successful, we knew we had to assign resources to the program. Our Hawk Academy was born. Our main concern was to ensure that the instructional systems we put in place would continue as we welcomed new staff members. The mentoring plan, we have found, provides a great opportunity to test possible up-and-coming administrators by giving some leadership responsibilities to our mentors.

A "train the trainer" session was done in early August, and all the mentors were present at the new teacher staff development. Each mentor had 3-4 teachers they were mentoring during the school year. We had activities every 6 weeks, coffee chats or lunch-and-learns, that allowed the whole group to come together and share best practices or offer conversations and/or reflections on the school year.

We have had several false starts to mentoring training in the past, but since we added a stipend, the program has been much more effective. We will do an exit survey as we finalize our year to ensure that we make adjustments to improve our program. So far, the feedback has been very positive.

A sound onboarding program with a mentor program ingrained will help with the sustainability of programming along with the retention of staff. The trend is so evident that the Texas Education Agency has rolled out a mentor incentive program established from our last legislative session. The sustainability of teachers in our profession has become so necessary due to the huge amount of turnover and ultimately to the changing of careers away from the teaching field.

Our mentoring program helps to strengthen our coaching for all teachers due to the development of our staff through our "train the trainer" program. We have worked to build a culture of trust and coaching among administration and peer to peer so that we can all learn from one another. So many times, the best teachers are present on your campus, but we do not provide opportunity to allow teachers to visit classrooms. This practice has helped to build capacity in our teachers, and they enjoy seeing their colleagues teach. Of course, at first, there is a little hesitation, but if a true coaching environment is built with support and trust, the possibilities will surprise you. We are seeing teachers who are proud to share ideas and who have ownership in their professional growth.

In summary, our journey to being the model of a learner-centered school has been very fulfilling for me and to our whole administrative team. Ideas or things that we reflected upon and thought might be a grand idea have been advanced three-fold once the teachers got involved and began to own the growth and culture. A recent teacher-led professional development may have been the best thing I have witnessed during my educational career. We may not amass a large bank account as Cornelius Vanderbilt did in the transportation business, but through some of the systems and culture built in our school over the last few years, I have a wealth that can't be bought with all the money in the world.

PROBLEM OF PRACTICE

This POP centers around *what I need* to sustain school systems. Our problem of practice is included to give you an example and to spark a thought that will lead to an action on your part. In the back of the book are pages for you to outline your problem of practice in your school. So, use our example as a catalyst or brainstorm with your team and identify a problem on your campus to focus on. Remember, focus on two to three important things and generate a team to help in this effort. Your problem of practice may take a few weeks or a few months, but most importantly, outline the problem and practice an actionable plan with your team to transform your school for a WIN!

Build a system to identify, implement and develop staff on an individualized basis. Student folders have been created to identify state standards deficiencies; a similar system should be created to develop teacher deficiency in identified standards.

Three years ago, our campus needed whole group improvement and understanding of our systemic processes. Through that whole group development and regular PLCs, our teachers have grown into effective teachers. The need currently is to further develop teachers in a precision method to ensure personal growth and development. It seems wasteful for the entire staff to sit through whole group staff development.

Focus Questions:

How can precision staff development be implemented?

How can we identify and track individual needs and growth?

What would be the best way to deliver independent staff development?

Could other teachers deliver staff development, and how would a schedule be developed?

Could teaming with neighboring schools be an effective process?

CHAPTER 12

WILL AND PASSION TO TRANSFORM

by *Stephanie*

"The height of the arrow determines how far you must pull back your bow."

The journey to becoming a learner-centered school is definitely just that: a journey. Furthermore, it is a difficult, time-consuming, and complex journey that, if done well, can truly transform your school and district. While we can't provide you with an exact step-by-step process or any single right way to make that transformation happen, there are some very definite systems that must be part of your non-negotiable processes. The first and most critical piece of transforming your school weighs heavily on the will and passion of every single faculty and staff member, including you and me as the school leaders. Every leader must possess the skills to lead, but we must also have a passion for seeking transformation and addressing the issues at hand. We all know what an amazing school looks and feels like, or we can envision that in our mind, but we often either don't know how to go about making that happen, or we lose our passion and will to bring about that change. We need to be leaders who step forward and say, "I want better for my students. I want better for the teachers and staff entering the doors each day. They all deserve the best."

I have some very good friends who are also school leaders. Each year, we take an annual girls' trip to spend a couple of days together. We schedule this time to fan the creative embers and to prepare for an amazing school year. These are not just getaways with my friends; rather, they are intentional journeys with the goal of refueling my energy for the start of a year. Before this particular school started this year, we all worked so late in the summer that we only had a short weekend together. The three of us, Lauren, Audrey, and myself, decided to go to Fredericksburg, Texas. On one of our workout mornings, we climbed Enchanted Rock. I think the word *rock* is misleading. It is a large granite mountain in which we had to make several rest stops on our climb until we reached the summit. When we reached the top, I saw some amazing views. There is something special about getting to the top of a peak. The sense of achievement is great for one, but equally important is the view. To stand on the top of a mountain and look at the 360-degree views with everything spread out around you is priceless. When you are standing on top of a large mountain, it truly gives you a good perspective. Something profound came to me that morning as we sat on top of the peak of the mountain.

Climbing a mountain or hill allows you to look down. As you scan the scenery, you begin to see a better way that you could have climbed up or you decide on a better route back down.

This simple outlook can be applied to all the leaders who are ready to tackle the transformation. There will be easier paths to travel. There will be mountains you have to conquer. We have no option but to climb the mountains in front of us. I know how hard it will be to do because I'm climbing them too. Some days you will feel defeated. Every step you are tackling is shaping you. If you get discouraged or tired, don't give up. Keep climbing the mountain. Don't worry about anyone who is farther along on this journey and reaching the top faster. This is your journey. Push yourself and give yourself the grace to rest, but keep climbing the mountain.

FOCUS ON THE TOP

We have to keep focusing on reaching the top. Once you secure your footing, start looking for another place to put your other foot. Trust the place you are standing. At this moment, you will know your own strength. Climbing the challenges of the school transformation will not only test your skillset but your physical and emotional strength too. It forces you to ask yourself, *who am I really? Do I have what it takes?* You will face mountains of pushback, criticism, and negativity, and days of that leave you trying to catch a breath, and you feel like you are losing your hold on the rocky mountain. At this moment, focus on the top.

Only uphill trails leave two choices: reach the top or turn yourself around. To reach the top, you will need the perseverance to keep putting one foot in front of the other. When your school reaches challenges, reach for the next place on the mountain and pull yourself up. There is no other way to reach the top of a mountain than to put in the effort step after step, step after step, and step after step.

School leadership and school transformation is a series of mountaintop moments. The journey is not always a straight path or an easy climb. There are many obstacles and chances to fall and lose your footing.

When we reach the top, it is definitely worth it. The achievement is fulfilling and motivating.

THE DRIVE TO WIN

Motivation is the most significant factor in success. Motivation will ensure maximum performance and give you the success you are seeking. The challenges of being a leader will take motivation to help you reach beyond the point at which our tasks are no longer fun and exciting. Let's face it: we will stare into the face of stress, burnout, and difficult tasks. These moments count. Staring these right in the eye will set you apart from the less successful leaders. There is no room for compromise. Wipe away all the excuses and distractions, and turn your back to the negativity. You are in control of your experience, your journey, and your circumstances. Doing something easy will never have an impact as significant as facing more difficult challenges. Your will to win will depend on your motivation. This will to win is found only within you.

DRAWING YOUR STRENGTH

How do you keep the motivation? Surround yourself with leaders who help you along the way. These people are those who thrive on the same desires to perform and to succeed, and they are willing to go through the transformation process. They are your education champions.

I was listening to a wonderful podcast one morning as I was preparing for work. The message caught my attention and made me stop and grab a piece of paper and write these words down.

> *"The height of the arrow determines how far you must pull back your bow."*

Without getting into physics and the science behind archery, let's take a minute and just ponder the quote. Pulling back on the strings of a bow makes the limbs of the bow bend. The farther you want the arrow to go, the farther you must pull back on the string. I'm not sure about you, but I have tried multiple times to pull back a bow. My husband is into archery and other outdoor activities. Therefore, I have unsuccessfully tried to pull back his bow. The bow is designed for him—for his strength and for his size. I'm not physically designed to pull his bow. This process makes me think about the pressures we face as educational leaders. We are not all designed to pull the weight of the things we face every day. Therefore, we need to surround ourselves with our educational champions who can help us pull the weight of the challenges. We all want success, but we all may not be prepared to face the pressures or the weight of the challenges. The right circle of friends and colleagues will push us and challenge us to be better. Draw on your strength and on the strength of others to allow your arrow to go farther. Seek out people who are relentless, positive, inquisitive, and dreamers of a better school and a better you.

ABOUT THE AUTHORS

S tephanie McConnell is a current principal in East Texas. She is an educational consultant and the face behind the website Principal Principles™.

Stephanie co-authored *Morale Magic*,™ which is a book filled with ideas and printables you can use to boost your school's morale. She was named the 2019 Principal of the Year by Texas Rural Education Association.

Her campus is a recipient of the 2019 National Blue Ribbon Award. The Blue Ribbon signifies exceptional student performance on state assessments.

M orris Lyon is a current superintendent and has served in educational leadership for the past 17 years. He has served in many statewide organizations, including the Texas Association of School Administrators, Texas Rural Education Association, Regional Education Service Center Advisory Boards, University Interscholastic League Waiver Board, and Western Governors University-Texas Advisory Board. He also serves as a clinical supervisor for Western Governors University's teacher field experience and educational leadership.

One of his district's campuses is a recipient of the 2019 Blue Ribbon School for closing the achievement gaps. Mr. Lyon was the 2014 Texas Rural Education Superintendent of the Year.

Problem of Practice (POP) Timeline

CIRCLE MONTH AND DATE OF MEETING

JAN FEB MAR APR MAY JUN JULY AUG SEPT OCT NOV DEC

1 2 3 4 5 6 7 8 9 10 11 12 13 14 15 16 17 18 19 20 21 22 23 24 25 26 27 28 29 30 31

MILESTONES:

WHAT HAPPENED THIS MONTH OR THIS WEEK:

OUR BIG WINS THIS WEEK/MONTH

1

2

REFLECT ON WHAT WAS LEARNED

WHERE IS YOUR FOCUS FOR THE NEXT WEEK OR MONTH? WILLL YOUR ORIGINAL FOCUS REMAIN OR IS AN ADJUSTMENT NEEDED?

REFLECTION

Printable Problem of Practice Pages for download here:
http://bit.ly/WINTIMEtransformyourschool

Problem of Practice (POP) Worksheet

Focus questions are general questions that will guide the discussion and probleming-solving process. In essence, the questions will guide your school to think about the challenges and problems the school is experiencing to help identify the root cause of the issue.

FOCUS QUESTIONS

? _____
_____

? _____
_____

? _____
_____

STAKEHOLDERS WHO HAVE DIRECT KNOWLEDGE OF THE PROBLEM:

When we achieve this POP, our school will improve in the following ways...
_____
_____

OUR NEXT STEPS:

WHAT RECOMMENDATIONS DOES THE TEAM HAVE FOR ADDRESSING THE POP?
- *Follow back in a week or month*
- *Clearly articulate the actions needed*
- *Build a collaborative culture for continous learning*
- *Develop and implement, system-wide strategies*
- _____
_____

Printable Problem of Practice Pages for download here:
http://bit.ly/WINTIMEtransformyourschool

Problem of Practice (POP) Worksheet

Problem of Practice (POP) identified

The end result of the POP is important to me because

OUR COMMITMENTS

COMMITMENT 1:

ACTIONS FOR COMMITMENT 1:

COMMITMENT 2:

ACTIONS FOR COMMITMENT 2:

COMMITMENT 3:

ACTIONS FOR COMMITMENT 3:

Printable Problem of Practice Pages for download here:
http://bit.ly/WINTIMEtransformyourschool

179

REFERENCES

Furtick, Steven (2020, January 6) Crushing: God Turns Pressure into Power with Bishop T. D. Jakes & Pastor Furtick (Audio podcast). https://podcasts.apple.com/us/podcast/elevation-with-steven-furtick/id216015753.

McConnell, Stephanie and Christine Bedre, Morale Magic™ Month-by-Month Guide to Boosting Morale, https://principalprinciples.lpages.co/morale-magic/ Published May 2018.

McConnell, Stephanie and Morris Lyon. "Transform Your School." 2019, http://bit.ly/transformyourschool Published October 2019.

.

CONTACT US

Stephanie from Principal Principles™
Twitter: @principalsteph1
Facebook:/principalprinciples
Instagram: @principalprinciples
Website: http://www.principalprinciples.net
EMAIL: principalprinciples@gmail.com

Morris Lyon
Twitter: @melyon60
Facebook:/morris.lyon.1
Instagram:@morris.lyon.1
EMAIL: morris.lyon.1@gmail.com

Made in the USA
Columbia, SC
15 June 2021